"This excellent woman's guide offers a much-needed message to the women I know. Regardless of age, relational brokenness leads to internal pain and a profound longing for wholeness. Kim Eckert uses sound psychological insight and biblical truth to provide tools for the journey of growing inward and outward. It's an amazing experience to accept and love the you God created through healing relationships."

JUDITH BALSWICK, marriage and family therapist, and coauthor of *A Model for Marriage*

"*Solid, thought-provoking, healing, challenging.* These four words describe my reaction to *Stronger Than You Think.* With the mix of the straightforward teacher and the insightful therapist, Kim Eckert gives women a book that speaks to our heads and our hearts. If it is time for you to take a positive, life-altering journey, this woman's guide is for you. I loved it."

JAN SILVIOUS, author of *Foolproofing Your Life* and *Big Girls Don't Whine*

"*Stronger Than You Think* offers to women and men sound theology and practical psychology on managing many of the perplexing dilemmas of being human. If you struggle with self-esteem, body image or relationship matters, then this book will help you to grow into the whole person that God created you to be."

VIRGINIA TODD HOLEMAN, professor of counseling, Asbury Theological Seminary

"This book will make you think and feel and grow. Kim Gaines Eckert draws on her extensive knowledge in Christian theology, spiritual formation and psychology, and yet makes it practical for everyday life. This is not just a helpful book for women, but also for the men who walk alongside women as friends, colleagues and lifelong partners."

MARK R. MCMINN, professor and author of *Finding Our Way Home: Turning Back to What Matters Most*

"The battleground for women's souls is in the mind. *Stronger Than You Think* equips women with the armor they need to combat society's messages, Satan's deceptions and our own internal misgivings."

CARA DAVIS, editor, *Radiant* magazine, and editorial director, RELEVANT Media Group

"Kim Eckert offers understanding, empowerment and hope to women struggling to overcome personal pain from the past and present. My clients will love this book."

CAROLYN KOHLENBERGER, executive director, Sunnyside Counseling Center, Portland, Oregon

"Every woman who worships the god of perfection can come to know the God of the universe while discovering the wonder of who God has made you to be."

STEPHEN ARTERBURN, author of *Healing Is a Choice*

Stronger Than You Think

BECOMING WHOLE WITHOUT HAVING TO BE PERFECT

a woman's guide

Kim Gaines Eckert

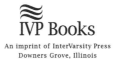

IVP Books

An imprint of InterVarsity Press
Downers Grove, Illinois

InterVarsity Press
P.O. Box 1400, Downers Grove, IL 60515-1426
World Wide Web: www.ivpress.com
E-mail: email@ivpress.com

InterVarsity Press® is the book-publishing division of InterVarsity Christian Fellowship/USA®, a student movement active on campus at hundreds of universities, colleges and schools of nursing in the United States of America, and a member movement of the International Fellowship of Evangelical Students. For information about local and regional activities, write Public Relations Dept., InterVarsity Christian Fellowship/USA, 6400 Schroeder Rd., P.O. Box 7895, Madison, WI 53707-7895, or visit the IVCF website at <www.intervarsity.org>.

All Scripture quotations, unless otherwise indicated, are taken from the Holy Bible, Today's New International Version.™ Copyright © 2001 by International Bible Society. All rights reserved.

Lyrics to the song "Tell Yourself," from the album Motherland, are written by Natalie Merchant ©2001 Indian Love Bride Music. Used by permission.

"When I Was a Boy," written by Dar Williams ©1993 Burning Field Music (ASCAP) administered by Bug. All rights reserved. Used by permission.

While the stories and examples in this book are based on real people and events, some names and identifying details have been altered to protect the privacy of the individuals involved.

Design: Cindy Kiple
Images: Rosanne Olson/Getty Images

ISBN-13: 978-0-8308-3373-3

Printed in the United States of America ∞

Library of Congress Cataloging-in-Publication Data

Eckert, Kim Gaines, 1974-
 Stronger than you think: becoming whole without having to be
 perfect: a woman's guide/Kim Gaines Eckert
  p. cm.
 Includes bibliographical references and indexes.
 ISBN-13: 978-0-8308-3373-3 (pbk.: alk. paper)
 ISBN-10: 0-8308-3373-0 (pbk.: alk. paper)
 1. Christian women—Religious life. I. Title.
 BV4527.E25 2007
 248.8'43—dc22

                                                                    2006038976

| P | 19 | 18 | 17 | 16 | 15 | 14 | 13 | 12 | 11 | 10 | 9 | 8 | 7 | 6 | 5 | 4 | 3 | 2 |
| Y | 22 | 21 | 20 | 19 | 18 | 17 | 16 | 15 | 14 | 13 | 12 | 11 | 10 | 09 | 08 | 07 | | | |

For the women who have entrusted me

with their stories of pain and brokenness.

Without their voices, I would have no story to tell.

And for my mother, Susan Hadley Gaines,

who is stronger than she thinks.

Contents

Acknowledgments

$\mathcal{I}$ am privileged to be in a profession in which people invite me into their inner lives, allowing me to walk alongside them through grief and loss, disillusionment and fear, brokenness and restoration. As women have sat in my counseling office and shared their stories with me over the years, I have longed to be able to provide them with a comprehensive resource that would address their concerns about body image and self-esteem, depression and anger, relational patterns and sexual wounds. Although names and personal details have been changed to protect their privacy, I have drawn heavily upon the experiences, struggles and insights of the women I have counseled and am profoundly indebted to them for their courage, honesty and willingness to allow me to walk with them for a season on their journeys.

I am also deeply grateful to InterVarsity Press, and especially to my editor Gary Deddo, for believing in me and the need for this book. Gary's theological insights have influenced my life in a personal way, and they are woven throughout this book. I am also indebted to my anonymous IVP readers, especially for their feedback on the *imago Dei* and embodiment issues. I am confident they will see their influence throughout.

This book began in a conversation with Mark McMinn in a small office at Wheaton College while I was still a graduate student. While talking about my desire to help women grow toward wholeness, Mark mentioned the idea of me writing a book on this topic. His encouragement and practical help have been invaluable throughout the writing process. Several years ago, Mark introduced me to another professional mentor, Bruce Narramore, whose thoughtful feedback also helped shape this book.

I am incredibly thankful for the supportive community I enjoy as a faculty member at Lee University, and I am especially grateful to Dr. Paul Conn for the presidential summer grant that assisted me during the writing of this manuscript.

Many other colleagues, friends and students have read and provided feedback on various parts of this manuscript, and I am indebted to each of them for their unique contributions: Beth Charrier, Vivian Cox, Carmen Daniel, Carolyn Eckert, Erica Fitzgerald, Jennette Leal, Gary Moon, Brittney Smith and Jennifer Swartout, as well as the students in my 2006 personality theory and psychology of women classes. I am especially grateful to Mr. Paul Wilhelm for his feedback on chapter eleven and for allowing me to share John's story. Brooke Kocher read a draft of the book with her women's small group at my church, North Shore Fellowship, and their feedback on the value of reading this book in community with other women motivated and encouraged me. Becky de Vaux, my research assistant, was willing to do whatever I needed, from hunting down books to formatting footnotes. Her editorial assistance and thoughtful reflections have been invaluable.

My parents and parents-in-law have provided many hours of childcare to help me finish this book. Jim and Jeanne Eckert have been as proud of me as any daughter-in-law could hope. I often thought of Jeanne while writing this book, because she models strength to all those around her—men and women alike. Since I was a child, my parents, Tom and Susan Gaines, have overwhelmed me with love, support and encouragement. My mother read every version of every chapter of this book and is hoping to singlehandedly put it on the bestseller list. I am lucky to have her as a cheerleader and friend.

I could not be more grateful for my sweet little boy, Thomas James. He is a miracle of love in every way, and he makes me want to be stronger than I think I am, to be a better mother than I think I can be. I am blessed to have a co-parent in my husband, Jeff, who is also a gifted psychologist. Jeff's clinical insights and interventions are reflected throughout this book. He has been my editor and proofreader, my sounding board and consultant, my chief marketer and biggest encourager. Through my relationship with Jeff, I am constantly challenged to encounter God, Jeff and myself in more authentic ways. For being my partner on this book, in parenting and in life, I am grateful.

And finally, this book was born out of a season of loss in my own life. I am forever grateful for a God who uses us in our brokenness—uses our most broken places to reach a hurting world.

PART ONE

Longing for Wholeness

1

Searching for Wholeness in Romance, Motherhood or Career

WHY A BROKEN WORLD LEAVES US DISAPPOINTED

*Girls have long been trained to be feminine at considerable cost
to their humanity. They have long been evaluated on the basis of appearance
and caught in myriad double binds: achieve, but not too much;
be polite, but be yourself; be feminine and adult; be aware of our cultural
heritage, but don't comment on the sexism. Another way to describe
this femininity training is to call it false self-training.
Girls are trained to be less than who they really are.
They are trained to be what the culture wants of its young women,
not what they themselves want to become.*

MARY PIPHER
REVIVING OPHELIA:
SAVING THE SELVES OF ADOLESCENT GIRLS

In 1996 a romantic comedy with a disturbing message to women de-
buted in movie theaters. Despite its underlying meaning, *Jerry Maguire*

was a blockbuster hit. The film centers on the life of sports agent Jerry Maguire, who ultimately marries his assistant—a single mother named Dorothy—for what he describes as "loyalty." Dorothy proclaims her love for Jerry at the outset of their romantic relationship, but Jerry is rather distant from Dorothy throughout the film. Finally acknowledging the difference in their feelings, Dorothy suggests they separate. In the climactic romantic moment of the film, Jerry returns to Dorothy and gives a long speech declaring his love. "You complete me," he tells her, and Dorothy accepts him immediately. "You had me at hello," she replies, even though he has been insensitive and inconsistent in his treatment of her throughout their relationship. Dorothy is desperate in her desire for wholeness, and she appears to believe that she can only find that sense of completion in romantic love.

Although it is unlikely that Dorothy will find a long-term sense of wholeness through a romantic relationship, many of us join her in this search for completion through love. We continue this search despite an underlying awareness that it will likely leave us dissatisfied. According to Henri Nouwen, "Many marriages are ruined because neither partner was able to fulfill the often hidden hope that the other would take his or her loneliness away. And many celibates live with the naïve dream that in the intimacy of marriage their loneliness will be taken away."[1]

Romantic love, however, is not the only path we search for wholeness. *If I could have a child to love I would feel like a complete woman,* or *If I was the perfect mother or wife, then I would be happy,* we might tell ourselves. Or perhaps, *If I could feel successful, like I was really good at something, then I would be satisfied.* We may search for wholeness in motherhood, a successful career or even Christian service, only to be disappointed when we have reached the goal and still feel like something is not quite right. Alternately, because of this internal sense of incompleteness, we may engage in destructive behaviors like substance abuse, excessive dieting or sexual promiscuity to fill that void.

---

[1] Henri Nouwen, *The Wounded Healer* (New York: Doubleday, 1972), p. 85.

"I am forty-five years old, and I have come to realize that I don't even know who I am," June told me in one of our early counseling sessions. "I know that I'm a mom and a wife. I do fine at my job and I have some friends, but somehow it's never quite enough. *I'm* never enough. I just want to feel whole." June's cry of the heart—that something is missing in her life, that she never feels like she is enough—is one I have heard from countless women, from those I counsel in my psychotherapy practice to students in my psychology classes. I hear about the pain of this struggle in conversations over coffee with girlfriends, and I recognize the ache of feeling that I am "never enough" in my own life.

I remember thinking as an adolescent how happy I would be when I got to drive a car or go to college. As a college student, I could not wait to graduate and get married. As a young married woman, I just knew that finishing graduate school and getting a great job would bring satisfaction. As a professional, motherhood became my next goal. And, in fact, I did love getting my driver's license, going to college, getting married and becoming a mother. I was grateful for each new experience and role, which made it all the more confusing and guilt-producing when I still felt like something was missing.

Pastors and Bible teachers encourage us to find our meaning and identity in Christ, and they remind us of the God-shaped hole inside us. When we try to fill that void with romance, success or even motherhood, we are bound to be disappointed. Only when we draw from the living well of God can we truly be satisfied and filled. Like many of the Christian women I know, I desperately want to be rooted in the love and protection of God. As much as I long for this in my own life, I get frustrated by my inconsistent devotional life, my selfishness and my desire to win the approval of others before God. If you are like me, you want to be filled up with God's presence and to find your peace and identity in him. When we don't see that happening in our lives, we add that to our guilt and self-condemnation.

This book is for women like June and me, women like my counseling clients, students and girlfriends—women who long for wholeness. It is for the women who have entrusted their stories to me and allowed me to walk alongside them on journeys in and through brokenness. This book is also for the countless women who may have never sought out counseling but resonate with June in their sense that something is missing or flawed within them.

WHY DON'T WE FEEL WHOLE?

Women feel broken in many ways. Often our relationships are one of the primary sources of our pain. We may have experienced a deep relational loss—and now we feel lost as well. Our current relationships may be hurtful or even abusive to us, or the wounds from a past relationship may continue to plague us. We may be struggling in a relationship with a spouse or significant other, mother or father, boss or coworker, son or daughter, friend or sibling.

Perhaps the relational brokenness is actually a byproduct of pain that is deep within us. We often feel deficient because of an underlying sense of inadequacy. We as females frequently possess endless lists of dislikes about ourselves: flabby thighs, boring personality, bad hair, oily skin, poor speaking abilities, minimal talent, no athletic ability, etc. When I asked June in one of our counseling sessions about her strengths, she struggled to come up with any. She was, however, able to describe in vivid detail the first time her mother asked her if she had gained weight, or the numerous times her father told her she wasn't smart enough to make it in college. We may have grown up hearing critical comments from parents, peers or siblings. As adults, we sometimes internalize those harsh statements and become our own biggest critics.

Even those of us who try to "do it all," being a loving wife, a dutiful mom, a productive career woman, a thoughtful friend and an active church member, are often plagued by the guilty sense that all our striving is never quite enough. We may look successful on the outside, but we feel conflicted in the inconsistency of the I-have-it-all-together image we portray to the world and the I'm-barely-holding-it-together reality that we live with on the inside.

In contrast, even with our greatest efforts, some of us can't portray that I-have-it-all-together image to the world. We may feel damaged all the way through. Perhaps we feel defeated in our depression, anger or anxiety. *If I could just kick this depression, I would feel whole again*, we may think to ourselves. Yet our efforts fail, and we are left feeling more depressed than ever. For others, the struggle is more subtle. We may not be dealing with issues like depression or abuse, yet we feel incomplete in ourselves and distant from God and others.

As much as women want to experience wholeness, it is a daunting task. It seems, at times, that we are surrounded by forces working against us in our desire to feel complete as women. Some of those forces are broad, rooted in the ways women have been oppressed politically and socially throughout history. Some are quite narrow, imposed through our families of origin and the messages we learned from our mothers and fathers, our grandparents and siblings. Some of the things that work against our natural desire to feel whole are cultural messages. When we turn on the television, we see women's bodies selling everything from cars to beer to jeans to perfume—not *women,* women's bodies. This is an important distinction and one that is so ingrained in our media that some of us have become numb to it. In advertising, women's bodies are split up into pieces, so we see sexualized photographs of a woman's lips or hips or breasts. Women's bodies are not women's whole selves. When women are valued for their beauty and sexual appeal to the neglect of their many other capacities and gifts, it fragments them. It teaches all women, both the fashion models and the media consumers, that women are important primarily for the sexualized *parts* of them, rather than for their *whole* selfhood.

SEARCHING FOR WHOLENESS IN THE CHURCH

Some of us may see the negative messages about women in the media and popular culture and turn to the church as a haven of safety. The church at its best reflects God's love and relational nature. As God the Father, Son and Holy Spirit are in constant fellowship with each other, so the church is called to reflect that fellowship and love. In such a God-reflecting community, the church provides a place of healing and restoration for both men and women. In an ideal Christ-empowered community, the hurting can find comfort, the rejected and ignored can find acceptance and love, and each individual's unique gifts are embraced and utilized in service of Christ and his kingdom. The church is not just a place to go but a place to *be*—to live out our callings and identities in what my pastor calls a "community of the broken." We are called to walk alongside other believers as we receive God's grace individually and corporately for every aspect of our lives. However, the church is filled with imperfect people just like you and me. This supportive community of love and respect is not always what we broken human beings offer or experience in the church. Consequently, a given local church can sometimes be a disconnecting place as well.

Despite the radical way in which Jesus ministered to and with women, women's roles in today's churches can be quite limited. Even though we read about the prophetess Anna (Luke 2:36), the disciple Tabitha (Acts 9:36) and the businesswoman Lydia (Acts 16:12-15) in the early church, many churches today do not allow women to hold positions of leadership. Shirley Gillett writes:

> The lessons the church and society taught me regarding my gender left indelible scars. Despite all the talk about "different" ministries for women, as opposed to "inferior" ones, it was pretty obvious to me, even as a young child, who was important to God. No one who says that men should do all the speaking, run things, and make all the decisions should really expect women not to get the message of their inferiority. I remember as a little girl crying myself to sleep at night, wondering why God didn't love me as much as a little boy.[2]

---

[2]Shirley Gillett, "No Church to Call Home," in *Women, Abuse, and the Bible,* ed. Catherine Clark Kroeger and James R. Beck (Grand Rapids: Baker Books, 1996), p. 107.

A woman who turns to the church for support in a disconnecting world may be personally gifted to teach or lead in some way, but in order to participate in the community of the church, she may have to deny those God-given skills. She may not even realize her gifts because of lack of consideration.

Women receive messages from the church not only by those things we are *not* allowed to do but also by the social activities and opportunities that *are* geared toward us. Most churches offer women's Bible studies or prayer groups. However, if we examine the activities specifically geared toward *social* connection, we often find an emphasis on stereotypically feminine activities, such as arts, crafts, cooking or having a mother's day out. Women usually organize these events and many women enjoy these activities; there is certainly nothing wrong with them. However, just like the media may teach that the value of a woman is found in her appearance, churches sometimes send a similar message: the value of a woman is in a *certain kind of woman*. Where are the activities for the woman who enjoys basketball and fishing but can't cook a meal or thread a needle? What kind of community does the middle-aged divorcee or the married but childless thirty-five-year-old woman find in the church? How are the gifts of the successful businesswoman or the human rights activist affirmed and celebrated in the church? The church can be a wonderful, healing place, and we are called to live life in the community of the church. However, churches are filled with broken people, and sometimes our churches can be a fragmenting influence as well.

WHAT IS WHOLENESS?

Thus far I have explored reasons we may not experience wholeness. We may feel less than whole when only certain parts of us are valued, like our appearance or sexuality, or when we are taught that we must be, act or look a particular way to be real women. When we internalize these messages and begin to believe them, we may find ourselves unwittingly playing a part in this struggle. For example, when I peruse *People* magazine while standing in line at the grocery store and find myself critiquing the featured female celebrity who has gained twenty-five pounds or has dropped so much weight that she is just skin and bones, I am contributing to the problem. The woman on that magazine is a real person—with many aspects to her personhood. When I overemphasize the importance of one aspect of her personhood, such as her body, I am not treating her as a whole woman.

What does it mean to treat someone as a "whole woman," or for you and I to *be* whole women for that matter? In light of this question, identifying what wholeness is *not* seems easy; it is a bit more challenging to define wholeness. Although the women I talk with sometimes describe wholeness as being something like perfection, I have found in my counseling practice that those who pursue perfection at all costs often suffer damaging consequences. For example, many anxiety disorders can be understood as a consequence of a pathological pursuit of perfection. Perfection implies an emphasis on performance and doing, but wholeness encompasses all of our being.

One of the definitions my college dictionary offers for being whole is "restored" or "healed," as in "She is a whole woman again."[3] Understood in this way, wholeness is a hope-filled concept. If wholeness is equivalent to perfection, then we are all destined for failure. We will never experience wholeness through sheer will and hard work. Our hope is that, despite our messy lives and our inability to live perfectly, we have a Savior who has already made us whole. In Christ we are being restored and healed. And even though we may not *feel* whole, wholeness is ultimately not about our feelings. Isn't that a relief? If I rely on my feelings to tell me whether or not I am whole, then my "wholeness" is likely to change with each success and failure. But wholeness is not based on our own subjective feelings. Rather, wholeness begins and ends with our hope in Christ and who we are in him. The reality is that even if our feelings lead us to believe otherwise, Christ has *already* restored and healed us in relationship to himself—so at the root of our very being he has already

---

[3]*The American Heritage Dictionary,* 2nd ed., s.v. "whole."

made us whole.[4] Who we are *is* who we are becoming in Christ. Even when I am inconsistent in my relationship with God and my pursuit of him, he is constant and faithful; I can rest in that truth.

Another definition my dictionary offers for wholeness is "healthy."[5] In contrast to being perfect, a whole woman, according to this definition, is a healthy woman. In the same way that we can improve our physical health through dietary or lifestyle changes, we can improve our emotional or relational health through practical life changes as well. Becoming whole does not mean being a perfectionist, but it does mean that we can *do* something. Although our culture, our families and even our churches may not always be affirming and empowering, we need not be in the victim role. Instead, empowered by the reality that Christ has already made us whole in relationship to him, we can be agents of change in our own lives and the lives of others. For example, we can look for ways to break maladaptive patterns in our thinking and our relationships; we can stop focusing on appearance—both ours and others—over other essential aspects of personhood. In short, we can actively pursue emotional, relational and spiritual health, trusting that "it is God who works in you to will and to act in order to fulfill his good purpose" (Philippians 2:13). When Jesus healed the paralyzed man, he told him to get up and take his mat and go home (Luke 5:24). Jesus did the healing work, but he also called the man to accept the gift, believe it and act on it. We, too, are called to believe and act on God's gift of wholeness and healing complete in Christ. Jesus gives us ways of being involved in what he's doing in our lives and to see that that wholeness shines forth more and more brightly in our lives.

Taken together, these two definitions illustrate the paradox of wholeness. Wholeness is already underway through Christ's redemptive work, as well as something that is not yet complete. Wholeness is a gift from God to be received, yet we can be actively involved in the working out

---

[4]See also T. F. Torrance, *The Mediation of Christ* (Grand Rapids: Eerdmans, 1983) for a theological discussion of Christ's mediatorial role on our behalf.

[5]*American Heritage Dictionary*, s.v. "whole."

of that gift. Wholeness is not merely a self-help program that we can achieve on our own; the paralyzed man didn't heal himself through his own will or efforts. However, it is also not something we passively absorb by osmosis; Jesus called the paralyzed man to receive the gift and get up and walk. Just as we are reconciled to God by grace through faith alone, we are also called to *live* holy lives. One way we can begin to live holy lives is through the pursuit of what the Hebrew prophets called *shalom:* "In the Bible, shalom means *universal flourishing, wholeness, and delight*— a rich state of affairs in which natural needs are satisfied and natural gifts fruitfully employed. . . . Shalom, in other words, is the way things ought to be."[6] Human beings, created in God's image, ought to be healthy, restored and healed.

This kind of *shalom* is something we experience when we live responsively and responsibly in God's kingdom. We experience wholeness when we live *responsively* to God and his good gifts. God has already restored us, healed us and made us whole through the redemptive work of Christ, and living responsively means that we trust in this foundational truth and accept God's gift of grace. We also experience wholeness when we live *responsibly,* when we take an active role in being good stewards of the gifts God has entrusted to us. Empowered by Christ and rooted in our knowledge of who we are as children made in God's image, we can make practical changes in our thoughts, behaviors and relationships to move toward health and wholeness.

WHOLENESS AND MEN

If wholeness means living responsively and responsibly, is that call to restoration, healing and health for women only? Of course not! Although this book is intentionally written for women, the longing for wholeness is a *human* longing, not a female one. The topics we will struggle with in this book, from negative self-talk to painful emotions, from

[6]Cornelius Plantinga Jr., *Not the Way It's Supposed to Be: A Breviary of Sin* (Grand Rapids: Eerdmans, 1995), p. 10.

sexuality to relational wounds, are in no way the sole domain of women. For example, when I examine how unrealistic images of perfection in the media affect a woman's body image, I am not suggesting this happens *only* for women and not for men. When my husband was in high school, he grew six inches in one year. As a sixteen-year-old, he was 6' 6" inches tall and weighed only 150 pounds! Despite his protein shakes and workouts, he could not add weight to his frame. If you think women are the only ones who worry about their appearance, just go to your local gym and ask yourself why so many men are there trying to lose weight, build mass or otherwise perfect their bodies.

As a therapist I have had the privilege of being a part of many people's journeys—both men and women—and the issues we will explore in this book are not exclusive to women. Although I am going to focus on how women might uniquely struggle with these things, I am not suggesting that men and women are psychological opposites. Although your local bookstore likely has piles of books exploring how men and women are as different as night and day (or Mars and Venus), social science research actually leads us to a different conclusion. The reality is that we aren't so different after all. Decades of research on psychological traits and behaviors indicates that there are actually very few consistent differences between the sexes and that males and females are much more alike than we are different.[7]

However, just because men and women have more similarities than differences does not mean that men and women *are* the same or experience life in exactly the same way. My oldest brother is nine years older than me, and he used to half-jokingly tell me we had different parents. He did not mean this literally; we are full siblings. Rather, he meant that the world I grew up in as the youngest of four was completely different

---

[7]See Mary Stewart Van Leeuwen, "What Do We Mean by 'Male-Female' Complementarity?" (paper presented at the annual meeting of the Evangelical Theological Society, San Antonio, Tex., November 2004) <www.eastern.edu/academic/trad_undg/sas/depts/psychology/mvanleeu/>; Mary Stewart Van Leeuwen, *Gender & Grace: Love, Work and Parenting in a Changing World* (Downers Grove, Ill.: InterVarsity Press, 1990), especially chap. 3; or M. Gay Hubbard, *Women: The Misunderstood Majority* (Dallas: Word, 1992).

than the world he grew up in as the firstborn. In a similar way, males and females sometimes feel as if the worlds we live in are vastly different. Consequently, the way in which males and females struggle with common human issues like self-worth and sexuality may differ.[8] For the purposes of this book, however, we will focus our energies on how women struggle *as women* and how we can begin moving toward wholeness and health.

A BLUEPRINT FOR THE JOURNEY: WHERE TO GO FROM HERE

I will focus on growing throughout the book, which involves looking forward and identifying ways to break patterns or make changes in the present and the future. However, I will also focus on healing in our journey toward wholeness, which often involves looking back at past wounds, trusting that God is moving us toward both growth and healing.

To that end, this book is divided into four parts. In the first part, "Longing for Wholeness," I will discuss reasons for our sense of brokenness and our desire for restoration. The theological concept that we have been made as relational beings in the image of God will be introduced as a guiding framework for our search for wholeness. In the second part of the book, "Growing Inward," I will explore how women often feel as though we are lacking in our minds, bodies, emotions and identities, as well as ways to grow toward wholeness in our inner lives. In the third part of the book, "Growing Outward," I will examine brokenness in our relationships and sexuality, and how we can grow toward wholeness in our lives with others. However, I will conclude this section of our study of wholeness by examining the paradox of finding wholeness even in our brokenness.

You may be inclined to believe that a book about wholeness will teach you how to "get it together" by the end of the book: have all the answers and know how to perfectly manage yourself, your thoughts, your relationships, etc. Please be warned that I make no such promise for this

---

[8]See also Hubbard, *Women.*

book! My concluding examination of brokenness is not meant to be a "bait and switch," in which your hopes that you would learn how to lead a happy, pain-free life are suddenly shot down. Instead, it is meant to be a reminder of the truth of the situation in which we find ourselves. The reality is that, in spite of our good intentions and genuine desire for wholeness, we mess up or bad things happen to us or to those we love. It is tempting to think of wholeness as the absence of brokenness—but brokenness is part of the human condition. We live in a fallen world where things are not the way they are supposed to be. Part of being whole is accepting that truth. Of course, brokenness is not the full story.

Wholeness is a paradox. Jesus is the perfect example of wholeness, though his life was characterized by suffering. True wholeness comes from joining with Christ in his suffering and finding healing in that. God redeems our brokenness through the work of Christ. God's intent is not to help us avoid pain and maximize pleasure; rather, God's intent is to grow us up in Christ. Therefore, I will conclude our study of wholeness by examining how we can continually receive from Christ and follow his example, allowing our own brokenness to help us reach out to the hurting in a real and genuine way.

GROWING IN COMMUNITY

As I will discuss in chapter two, God has created us for relationships, and all of the ideas and suggestions in this book are best explored in the context of a safe and committed relationship (or relationships). Recently a women's small group at my church read the manuscript for this book. The women in the group are diverse in occupation and age (ranging from early twenties to early sixties), and each week they read a chapter or two of the book and met together to discuss it. After they had finished the book, I attended one of their groups for them to give me feedback and tell me about their experiences. "Please tell your readers this is a book meant to be read in relationship with others," one of the members urged me. "It wouldn't have been the same book for me without the community experience." Women in the group commented on how the differing experiences and perspectives of the other group members challenged them to think about and reflect on the ideas here in ways they would not have thought about on their own.

In the last section of the book, "Growing in Community," I provide a guide for you to engage in this journey toward healing and wholeness in community with a small group, partner, mentor, counselor or trusted friend. This book is not intended to substitute for professional counseling when it is necessary for things like depression, anxiety or abuse. Rather, the ideas presented here are intended to be conversation starters, leading to deeper relationships—not as a replacement for relationships. The idea of reading a book like this with a friend or partner may seem intimidating or even threatening. As one of the group members at my church said, "I was afraid to share my painful memories and feelings with others." However, as she began to understand how God has made us in his image for relationships, she said, "I began to realize the healing offered by God is only possible *in* and *through* a community, and my reluctance to share such a journey with others was actually self-defeating." If you will allow God to help you be vulnerable and join with others on this journey, I wholeheartedly believe you will open yourself up to the possibility of more significant growth and healing than you could find individually.

At their best, relationships bring value and meaning to the events of our lives. However, they can also bring disabling and long-lasting pain. As a clinical psychologist, I believe that most, if not all, of our emotional problems are either rooted in or affected by personal relationships. Consequently, healing from emotional pain will be most effective when it is done in the context of interpersonal relationships. As relational beings made in God's image, we grow best in relationship with others. When my accountability partner and I meet for breakfast on Fridays and talk about how pride and selfishness are keeping us from God and others, the changes I make in my life are rooted in and grow out of my relationship with her. Without that conversation with a trusted friend, I would be less likely to pay attention to my selfishness and the call to live like Christ—

sacrificially and unselfishly. Relationships are the context in which growth and change takes place.

When I see a woman in counseling, I often ask her to reflect on a number of thoughts or questions during the time between our sessions. In this way, she can do the work of therapy all week outside my office. The last section of the book is not merely a study guide. Rather, it is filled with the kind of questions I ask the women I counsel, questions for discussion and reflection, as conversation starters, as guidelines for sharing and as a framework to assist you on your own personal journey toward wholeness. Although these questions can be used for personal contemplation or journaling, they are meant to be examined with others in the context of secure and trusting relationships. As you read through these chapters, some of them may be more applicable to you than others. My prayer is that you would embark on this healing journey in community with a partner or mentor. Together you can exchange ideas, reflect on your own experiences and be encouraged to persevere when you feel like giving up.

Reading this book in community not only allows someone else to encourage you, but it opens the door for God to use you in another person's life. One of the women in the small group sent me an e-mail after they completed the book, and she put it this way: "I had no idea of the role I was to play in the lives of the other women in the group, nor they in mine. Part of that discovery set me free to realize the kind of woman God has called me to be, not simply *me*, but *me as part of a community,* called to be a place of healing and hope for others."

A Word of Encouragement for the Journey

When I was in college, I began running. Just writing that sentence still brings me joy, because let me tell you: I was *not* a runner. In fact, I hated running and dreaded gym class for as long as I can remember. But due to some changes in my life, I decided to tackle running during my senior year in college. Eventually, I even ran a few road races, for which I trained with a friend who had been a cross-country runner.

Training was really helpful, because when I started running I had no idea what I was doing. Basically my thought process went something like this: *Running is running: just put one foot in front of the other. If you get to the end, it's a miracle anyway. Who cares how you get there?* While it did always feel like a miracle when I reached my destination, I found that it was often pretty hard to get there because of the way I ran. I didn't drink enough liquids, I didn't set my feet correctly, I forgot to breathe or my breathing was too fast, I tensed all the muscles in my shoulders and arms, I turned my whole body from side to side when I ran, and I took really short strides. As a result, I got tired very quickly, had limited endurance and would struggle through numerous muscle cramps on any given run.

However, when I started training with my friend, my whole running experience was transformed. He taught me to correct my stride and count out my breathing. He suggested that I imagine holding a penny between my fingertips to keep me from making fists and punching my arms from side to side, which had previously tired me out in minutes. I still use the techniques he taught me when I go jogging. My friend didn't run my races for me, and he couldn't make me into a better runner if I wasn't willing to do the work. He did, however, give me the tools to make my journey an easier and more productive one.

You, too, are on a journey, and it is yours alone. No one else can run it for you. However, as a Christian psychologist, I can offer tips, suggestions, activities or images that may assist you on your journey. Each chapter of this book concludes with a "Tools for the Journey" section. Some of these "tools" come from personal experience, some from research and reading, others from my counseling practice. I may offer suggestions for recognizing ways in which you're slowing yourself down, causing yourself needless exhaustion, or experiencing unnecessary or inappropriate pain on your journey.

However, as much as I believe in the benefits of counseling, please do not read this book in the hope that a psychological technique will give you a quick-fix healing. True wholeness is found in one place, and that is Christ alone. But God also uses human care and human wisdom to assist us on our journeys. I was helped along on my running journey by my friend's training before the race, but I was also helped by the volunteers handing out needed water and shouting words of encouragement during the race. God speaks to us through his Word, through prayer and worship, but he also speaks to us through human agents—coaches and cheerleaders on our journeys. My hope is that I can be a little of both for you during this journey toward wholeness.

Any woman who desires wholeness and is willing to engage on a journey toward emotional healing and wholeness is stronger than she thinks. The women I see in counseling are consistently stronger than they think, and part of the joy of counseling is walking alongside them as they rediscover that inner strength. By embarking on this kind of journey, you are brave enough to admit that something is not right. You are courageous enough to try to change. This is an incredibly vulnerable position, and yet the women I counsel—and I also believe you who are reading this book—will do it anyway. You truly are stronger than you think.

2

Finding Wholeness in Our True Identity

RELATIONAL BEINGS MADE IN GOD'S IMAGE

Behind the dirty curtain of our painful symptoms there is something
great to be seen: the face of Him in whose image we are shaped.

HENRI NOUWEN
THE WOUNDED HEALER

ou have amazing worth and value. You are special and unique. Does this
sound like the introduction to one of countless "feel good" self-help
books on your local bookstore's shelves? In a popular self-esteem book
for women, readers are warned against trying to find worth in relationships, work or motherhood. Instead, "we need to believe that our life has
some intrinsic meaning and need not be justified by anyone or anything
external."[1] Women do need to stop looking for value solely in activities
and accomplishments, but where do we find that "intrinsic meaning"?
Does simply existing, living, breathing give us value? As a Christian, the
answer to this question is a resounding yes!

---

[1]Linda Tschirhart Sanford and Mary Ellen Donovan, *Women and Self-Esteem: Understanding and Improving the Way We Think and Feel About Ourselves* (New York: Penguin Books, 1985), p. 348.

Lillian, a forty-two-year-old woman I worked with in counseling, grew up in a conservative Christian home. As a child, her church's teaching centered around the fact that we are utterly sinful creatures from birth. Regardless of the number of Sunday school classes Lillian taught or volunteer activities she coordinated, Lillian struggled with a chronic sense of guilt. She could always do more, she reasoned. If Lillian was affirmed for her hard work at church or in the community, she tended to minimize her efforts. Sometimes a church member or friend complimented Lillian's character, her kindness or generosity; Lillian almost felt like just listening to those affirmations was a sin. "I don't want to be prideful," she told me. Her childhood teaching had drilled her utterly sinful nature into her psyche. She was not confused about her badness. Lillian was less aware, however, of her goodness.

When Lillian's teachers and parents taught her that she was a fallen creature, they were absolutely correct—we are all sinful. However, focusing exclusively on our sin nature is like tuning in to a film sequel before ever watching the original. Before sin entered the world, God created human beings in his own image. We *are* fallen people, and that status has brought with it innumerable problems, but we are *still* made in the image of God. And even more, we can be restored and healed and made whole again through the person of Jesus Christ. Lillian, like all of us, is sinful. However, she is also a wonderful woman made in God's own image, restored and renewed through Christ's redemptive work.

In this chapter, I am going to dive into the theological and biblical truths that will provide the foundation for our journey toward wholeness. In the theology of the *imago Dei* (that's Latin for "image of God"), we will explore the reality that we have been made whole in God's image and that God has wired us so intensely for relationships that we find our being in and through relationships. I will explore how this looks in the life of Jesus and what the theological blueprint of the image of God means for our journey. The image of God is who we are—it's where our journey toward wholeness begins. The image of God is also who we are becoming—it's where our journey toward wholeness is taking us.

MADE WHOLE IN GOD'S IMAGE . . . RESTORED IN CHRIST

Then God said, "Let us make human beings in our image, in our likeness, so that they may rule over the fish in the sea and the birds in the sky, over the livestock and all the wild animals, and over all the creatures that move along the ground."

So God created human beings in his own image,
 in the image of God he created them;
  male and female he created them. (Genesis 1:26-27)

We have been formed and made in God's own image and likeness.[2] Our whole person is made in God's image, not just a part of us. Some theologians have emphasized certain aspects of what it means to be made in the image of God, like our ability to reason or our moral conscience. Even though these are important elements of being created in God's image, they are just that—elements. It is our whole personhood and our whole self that is created in God's image. As people made in God's image, we have a unity and harmony of every aspect of our being—including the relationship between our innermost and outermost selves (our souls and bodies). This means that *God made us whole.* Although we are fallen and broken creatures, we were created whole, and Christ has renewed that wholeness in us through his redemptive work.

Because of the Fall, however, we often do not *feel* whole, as discussed in chapter one. Lillian, for example, described a feeling of aching emptiness that she tried to fill with service to her church and family: "It seems like I can never do enough for my husband or my children," she told me. "I always think that the next thing I do will make me feel like I'm doing okay as a wife or mother, that it will make me feel complete.

---

[2]For further reading on the *imago Dei*, see Anthony A. Hoekema, *Created in God's Image* (Grand Rapids: Eerdmans, 1986); Stanley Grenz, *The Social God and the Relational Self: A Trinitarian Theology of the Imago Dei* (Louisville, Ky.: Westminster John Knox Press, 2001), especially chap. 5; Jack O. Balswick, Pamela Ebstyne King and Kevin S. Reimer, *The Reciprocating Self* (Downers Grove, Ill.: InterVarsity Press, 2005); Karl Barth, *Church Dogmatics* 3/2, trans. H. Knight, G. W. Bromiley, J. K. S. Reid and R. H. Fuller (Edinburgh: T & T Clark, 1960); Colin E. Gunton, *The Promise of Trinitarian Theology* (Edinburgh: T & T Clark, 1991).

But no matter what I do, it's never enough." Many of us, like Lillian, do not feel whole. In other words, we do not experience *shalom*.

Whereas *shalom* is the epitome of the wholeness and unity of human beings in right relationship with God and creation, sin is that which damages or breaks *shalom*.[3] Because of sin, our relationships have been twisted and distorted—from the inner relationship between body and spirit, to interpersonal relationships between husband and wife or parent and child, to the broader relationships between races and nations, humans and nature. The impact of sin is felt in every corner of our world. Despite the presence of sin, we were made whole persons with unity and harmony, created in the image of God. In other words, we were made for *shalom*. Because of sin (both ours and others), we do not always experience wholeness in our own lives nor do we always help others to experience it in their lives. But God has graciously preserved and maintained his original purpose for his creation: for us to be images that reflect the very life and character of God.

In spite of our shalom-breaking, Jesus offers the unbelievable hope that, even when our feelings tell us otherwise, the wholeness we were created in by God is actually maintained and restored in us through Christ. As theologian James Torrance writes, "In *him* and through *him* we are renewed by the Spirit in the image of God."[4] He has restored that wholeness in us through his redemptive work. Lillian, in her longing for wholeness, was trying to make herself complete through a flurry of activities that were leaving her exhausted. Jesus gently calls Lillian and us to be joined to him, and to let go of our futile attempts to make *ourselves* whole. Instead, we can rest in the work he has already completed in us. "Come to me, all you who are weary and burdened, and I will give you rest," Jesus invites us. "Take my yoke upon you and learn from me, for I am gentle and humble in heart, and you will find rest for your souls" (Matthew 11:28-29).

---

[3]Cornelius Plantinga Jr., *Not the Way It's Supposed to Be: A Breviary of Sin* (Grand Rapids: Eerdmans, 1995), p.14.

[4]James B. Torrance, *Worship, Community & the Triune God of Grace* (Downers Grove, Ill.: InterVarsity Press, 1996), p. 14, italics mine.

BEINGS-IN-RELATIONSHIP

As individuals made in God's image, we have been made whole. This doesn't mean, however, that we are meant to do life on our own. But, you may ask, doesn't *wholeness* imply that we are complete in and of ourselves? In stark contrast to this kind of thinking, Christian wholeness is found not individually but through community—first with God and then with others. The way we receive and experience wholeness, or *shalom*, takes place in the context of relationships with God and others.

As God is an inherently relational being, he has made us inherently relational beings as well: "To be human is to be in relationship with another."[5] God stated, "Let *us* make human beings in *our* image," not "Let *me* make human beings in *my* image." God is, within the trinity of the Father, Son and Holy Spirit, constantly in fellowship with himself. As Stanley Grenz writes, "The three members of the Trinity are 'person' precisely because they are persons-in-relationship."[6] In the same way, we are human beings because we are beings-in-relationship. In other words, my being in relationship (e.g., with God, my family members, my friends, my church members and my neighbors) is not just a bonus or something I may or may not choose to pursue. Rather, there is no "me" outside of relationship. The question is *how* we will be in relationships, not *whether* we will be in relationships. Relationships, therefore, are not just a good thing to have in life but are essential to any life we do have.

One way to think of our relational identity is in a double orientation with both a vertical and horizontal axis.[7]

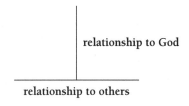

relationship to God

relationship to others

[5]Balswick, King and Reimer, *Reciprocating Self,* p. 36.
[6]Grenz, *Social God and the Relational Self,* p. 332.
[7]Gunton, *Promise of Trinitarian Theology,* p. 116.

We have been created first for relationship with God. This is the vertical axis of our lives and the foundation upon which all other relationships are built. Because of sin, that vertical relationship is sustained by the redemptive work of Christ, in whom "we live and move and have our being" (Acts 17:28). In our relationship with God, we discover both who God is and who we are. For it is only in relationship to our Creator and Redeemer that we can learn who he has created us to be. "In our relationship with God we not only encounter the living God, but we become most fully ourselves."[8]

In becoming a parent I discovered God and myself in a new way. As I awaited the birth of my son and began to think and feel more like a mother, I gained a greater understanding (however small it still is) of God's love for us. At the same time, I discovered in myself a capacity to love beyond that which I knew I was capable of. Through my relationship with God and his gift of my son, I learned more about God and became more fully aware of who God has created me to be.

God has created each of us to be unique selves with gifts, capacities, abilities, preferences and talents. These gifts are given to us for a particular purpose: to participate in right relationships with God and others. How we use these gifts can either reflect the truth of who we are in Christ or deny it. Lillian, a unique woman made in God's image, was well-respected by her family and friends, yet she often could not see her own gifts. Even more, many of her capacities were left unused. For example, Lillian allowed her husband to make almost all of the decisions in their marriage, from the houses they bought to the movies they watched. Lillian was gifted with intelligence and the ability to make decisions and share her opinions, but the gift's power remains dormant, hidden and undeveloped when it is not used. When we neglect or misuse the gifts God has given us, or when we fail to discover who God has created us to be, we reflect a cloudy, or perhaps even distorted, image of God in us.

---

[8]Balswick, King and Reimer, *Reciprocating Self,* p. 39.

Not only have we been created for relationship with God, we have also been created for relationships with others. This is the horizontal axis of our lives, born out of our vertical relationship to God and mediated through Christ. In contrast to the individualistic message of our culture that we can and must live autonomously, God created us for community. Theologian Karl Barth pointed out that God is the author and creator not only of human beings but also of the human relationship: "As God creates both man and woman, he also creates their relationship, and brings them together."[9] As beings-in-relationship, we discover both others and ourselves in the contexts of our relationships. For example, in my relationship with my closest girlfriend, I am constantly learning about her character and personality, her interests and abilities, but I am also learning about myself through our relationship. By seeing myself through her eyes, I get a better understanding of my unique strengths and weaknesses.

Relationships that reflect the image of God are characterized by freedom—the freedom to be who we are and to allow others to be who they are. Because sin has twisted and distorted this relational need, some of us tend to lose ourselves in relationships. Lillian wanted other people to be happy at all costs, and she frequently ignored her own thoughts and feelings in an effort to maintain relationships. Lillian began a pattern early in her marriage of deferring nearly all decisions to her husband. Rather than speak up with her husband or her friends, Lillian would do whatever was needed to keep the other person happy. In an effort to maintain relationships, Lillian tended to lose her unique identity in those relationships. Intimate relationships that reflect God's character should preserve and protect our individuality and differences, not smother or ignore them.

In contrast to Lillian, sometimes we do not give others the freedom to be themselves in relationships. For example, I am energetic and outgoing. I love parties and meeting new people. My husband, on the other

---

[9]Barth, *Church Dogmatics* 3/2, p. 291.

hand, is calm and relaxed. He attends parties only if necessary, because he much prefers getting to know people one-on-one rather than in a large group atmosphere. Although I know and love this about my husband, I do not always treat him in a way that accounts for this difference. When we are driving home from a party and I critique him for not being "social" enough, I am not giving him the freedom to be himself—a unique man made in God's image with special gifts, abilities and characteristics. To be a human being in relationship is "to be given space to be—by others in community."[10] Authentic relationships that reflect God's nature are characterized by unity in diversity. God created my husband and me in different ways, and when I do not give him the space to be himself, I do not honor the differences God created.

Just like the self-help books say, we *are* special! But our value is not in some inherent goodness we have achieved by our own merit. Rather, our worth is firmly planted in our identity as children of God, made in his image. What's more, we come to see and understand our value and uniqueness only in relation to another—to God or to other people. In the context of relationships, we discover God, others and ourselves. God's purpose is for us to *be* and *become* more than what we are by ourselves, and he helps us achieve this in and through our relationships with him and others. In this sense, the image of God "is human life directed to an end. The image is not a static possession, but comes to be realized in the various relationships in which human life is set."[11] Through our relationships with God and others, we are changed and transformed. This is why this book is designed to be read and reflected on in community. Relationships are not just optional; instead, they are the context in which our journeys toward wholeness and healing take place.

Recently, I took a group of students on a study abroad trip. One night eight of us ended up squeezed into a tiny student hotel room, talking

---

[10]Gunton, *Promise of Trinitarian Theology,* p. 117.
[11]Ibid., p. 119.

into the early hours of the morning. As the young men and women in that room shared their stories—stories of shame and guilt—I was overwhelmed by God's presence. As individual students poured out their hearts, the other men and women in the room *really* listened. Genuine care was evident in what was said and in what was left unsaid (jokes, blaming, critical comments, pat answers). I watched as the men and women in the room were moved to tears by the gut-wrenching pain others had experienced. I walked away from that conversation with a new picture of what God's love and grace looks like in action, and I was not alone. For the rest of the trip, those students referred back to that night. Neither my students nor I would have experienced the growth we did in that hotel room at 3 a.m. *outside of our relationships* with each other. This doesn't mean that we became dependent or clingy or lost our unique identities in those relationships. Rather, it means that we changed and grew and healed in and through those relationships.

PUTTING FLESH ON THE IMAGE OF GOD: JESUS

Thus far, I've written a lot about a heady theological concept, the *imago Dei,* and perhaps you are wondering what this actually *looks* like. When I am grading students' papers, I will sometimes write, "Put some flesh on this!" next to a complex idea they are trying to explain. We all respond to, connect with and understand things more when we are given practical examples or illustrations. And thankfully, God has provided us with the perfect living example of what it means to faithfully reflect God's image (his unity in diversity, his oneness with God and human beings). That example is found in the person of Jesus Christ.

In Jesus, we find the perfect example of what it means to live in community. Through the incarnation, Jesus is both fully God and fully human. He is one with God and one with humanity. As we are joined with Christ, we are able to be unified with God and other believers. God calls us to live our lives in community with other believers—not just with our family members and friends. Christ is the foundation of the church, which is intended to be a sign "not only of God's way of being in creation but of the dynamic of the eternal, triune God."[12] As such, the church is meant to be a community in which we corporately reflect God's holy, loving, relational nature.

Where we are sinful, Jesus is sinless. Where we are faithless, Jesus is faithful. Where we are hurtful, Jesus is healing. Sin has corrupted and distorted our world—it has corrupted and distorted *us.* Yet Jesus came to take away the sin of the world and reverse the effects of the Fall. This is the redemptive work of Christ "who gave himself for us to redeem us from *all* wickedness" (Titus 2:14, italics mine). Sin is "a parasite, a vandal, a spoiler,"[13] but Christ restores and renews every part of us. Jesus brought the good news that we have been made whole again, that our relationship to God has been restored and our relationships with others have been given a whole new basis through the working of Christ. Ultimately, Jesus brought hope—hope that we can know God as he is and know ourselves as we truly are, made in God's own image.

Because of Christ's redemptive work, wholeness is not something to just strive toward on our own. Rather, wholeness is a gift that has been won for us through Christ's sacrifice. Even when we were sinful, Christ redeemed us: "But because of his great love for us, God, who is rich in mercy, made us alive with Christ even when we were dead in transgressions—it is by grace you have been saved" (Ephesians 2:4-5). It is by grace we are saved, but it is also by grace that we *grow* and *heal* and *mature.* Jesus mediates every part of our lives with God—not just our conversion experiences. The undeserved blessing in this is that we can *rest* on our journey, knowing we can't "get there" on our own, knowing wholeness and healing is not something we attain through hard work. Rather, as we share in Christ's life and death, his suffering and sacrifice, we experience his wholeness.

We are like toddlers who are just learning to walk, clinging to our parents' hands as we stumble along.[14] By living *responsively,* we grasp the

---

[12]Grenz, *Social God and the Relational Self,* p. 336.
[13]Plantinga, *Not the Way It's Supposed to Be,* p. 199.
[14]Thomas F. Torrance, *The Mediation of Christ* (Grand Rapids: Eerdmans, 1983), p. 93.

strong hand held out to us and accept the gift of God's grace and the work that is already completed in us through Christ. By living *responsibly,* we take one wobbly step after another. We take hold of the life to which God has called us (1 Timothy 6:12). As we stumble along, we find our confidence in the strong hand of our Redeemer, knowing that "he who began a good work in you will carry it on to completion until the day of Christ Jesus" (Philippians 1:6).

BEING AND BECOMING

At the very beginning of our journey is set this foundational truth: *the image of God is who we are.* The image of God is first and foremost a structure; it is the core of our selfhood and our very being. To be human is to bear the image of God. You *do* have inherent worth and value, regardless of your appearance, talents, relationships, work, etc. You have inherent worth and value as a being-in-relationship, created in God's own image. The adage (or is it a bumper sticker?) states, "God made you, and he doesn't make mistakes," and this is true. You were created a unique and whole person in God's image: "Each of us is unrepeatable, a unique bearer and reflector of the glory of God. Nobody else can reflect God's light in exactly the same way as you can."[15] Your mind, body and spirit in unity reflect and mirror God. C. S. Lewis put it this way: "He makes each soul unique. If he had no use for all these differences, I do not see why He should have created more souls than one."[16] God has preserved us in and through the Fall. His purpose for us remains in force—to be people who reflect the loving relational nature of God revealed in Christ. Sin has not undone what God has created and redeemed.

At the conclusion of our journey is another foundational truth, inviting and encouraging us to keep going: *the image of God is who we are becoming.* The Bible tells us to "live a life worthy of the calling you have received" (Ephesians 4:1). The image of God is not only a structure; it is

---

[15]Cornelius Plantinga Jr., *Engaging God's World: A Christian Vision of Faith, Learning, and Living* (Grand Rapids: Eerdmans, 2002), p. 40.
[16]C. S. Lewis, *The Problem of Pain* (New York: Macmillian, 1962), p. 147.

also a *calling*. Because we are broken and fallen creatures, we are unable to perfectly reflect God. However, we are also joined with Christ. "Jesus Christ is our human response to God. Thus we appear before God and are accepted by him as those who are inseparably united to Jesus Christ."[17] The task of the Christian, then, is to participate in the continuing life and ministry of Christ, who is the perfect "image of the invisible God" (Colossians 1:15). As a structure, the image of God is a noun; as a calling, the image of God is best understood as a verb. For example, "We no longer *image* God as we should," Anthony Hoekema writes, "we are now being enabled by the Spirit to *image* God more and more adequately; some day we shall *image* God perfectly."[18] The image of God is not just who we are; the image of God is also who we are becoming.

Human beings are on the way to something else—to someone else. God is growing us and changing us as he prepares us to be his bride. "Now we see but a poor reflection as in a mirror," the apostle Paul writes, "then we shall see face to face. Now I know in part; then I shall know fully, even as I am fully known" (1 Corinthians 13:12). The kingdom of God is both now and not yet. As relational beings made in God's image, we are already fully known by Christ. One day, however, we will meet God face to face. On that day, we will finally have the ability to fully know God and others. God calls us now, to live responsively and responsibly as he grows us up into Christ.

One way I wrap my mind around the complexities of this theological concept is to think about my role as a mother. When I had my son, I became a mother. Being a mother is *who I am;* it is a structure. No matter what happens to me or to my son in this life, I will be a mother. No one can change that or take that away. At the same time, I am continually growing in my capacity to be a good mother. I did not immediately know how to perfectly mother my son when he was born. I am constantly learning—from mistakes, from other mothers, from parenting books,

---

[17]Torrance, *Mediation of Christ,* p. 90.
[18]Hoekema, *Created in God's Image*, p. 28.

from my relationship with God and from reading his Word. In all these ways, being a mother is *who I am becoming;* it is a calling. I already am a mother, but I am also constantly growing in my capacity to be a good mother, the kind of mother my son needs.

In a similar way, I am already made in the image of God; it is my core identity and no one can change that truth. I *am* an image-bearer of God—how amazing! At the same time, I am constantly growing in my ability to receive God's grace in order to image him more accurately to the world around me. In this way, I am *becoming* an image-bearer as I am learning to join with Christ and share in his life and death.

We have been made in God's image. Therefore, we have inherent worth and value. Throughout this book, we will explore *who we are* as women made whole and unified in all aspects of our selfhood: mind and body, emotions and sense of self, relationships and sexuality. Many of us, however, feel damaged in these various aspects of our selfhood. Therefore, we will also examine *who we are becoming* in our search for wholeness. Christ has already done the work and made us whole. Who we are *is* who we are becoming in Christ. Through our union with him, we receive more and more fully his wholeness, which then manifests itself in our lives and relationships as we live responsively and responsibly.

PART TWO

Growing Inward

3

Learning to Use Your Voice

RECOVERING FROM THE
NEGATIVE MESSAGES OF GIRLHOOD

Captain Harville: *"I do not think I ever opened a book in my life which had not something to say upon woman's inconstancy. Songs and proverbs all talk of woman's fickleness. But perhaps you will say, these were all written by men."*

Anne: *"Perhaps I shall. Yes, yes, if you please, no reference to examples in books. Men have had every advantage of us in telling their own story. Education has been theirs in so much higher a degree; the pen has been in their hands. I will not allow books to prove anything."*

JANE AUSTEN
PERSUASION

$\mathcal{I}$n the 1997 film *As Good as It Gets* a flighty female receptionist asks Melvin, the character played by Jack Nicholson, how he writes women so well. Melvin responds, "I think of a man, and I take away reason." Unfortunately, Melvin's message regarding a woman's mental capacities is one we often receive in the media. Take, for example, the horror film genre. When a woman is being chased by a plodding but treacherous killer, where does she inevitably run? The woman predictably chooses the worst of all options by running upstairs, effectively trapping herself and causing her own demise. What is the hidden message in this scenario? Women are dimwitted, and if their silly choices cause them problems, it is their own fault. Or perhaps we have learned about women from romances or dramas, in which women are seemingly always getting themselves into perilous situations from which they need rescuing by a strong and attractive male.

The media, however, is not the originator of these messages about women's reasoning skills. We receive messages about our thinking abilities from many sources, including parents, teachers, textbooks, literature, music and peers, and it begins long before adulthood. In this chapter I will examine how, as girls, we learn that a female's value lies not in her intellect but in her appearance and ability to please others. Consequently, many females' thoughts and voices are silenced during girlhood. I will examine ways to begin using that lost voice, since we have been made with minds worth listening to and can mirror God more accurately when we use them to foster authentic relationships with God and others.

WHAT WE LEARNED IN SCHOOL

The American Association of University Women (AAUW) documented some of the messages girls receive about their rational abilities as well as the impact of those messages in their study "How Schools Shortchange Girls." Through classroom videotape analyses and a national survey of 3,000 boys and girls between the ages of nine and fifteen, disturbing results were found regarding what girls were seeing, reading and hearing in school.[1] The AAUW study reports that as girls progress through school, their standardized test scores drop, as well as their interest and

---

[1]For further reading on the 1992 AAUW study, see Peggy Orenstein, in association with the American Association of University Women, *Schoolgirls: Young Women, Self-Esteem, and the Confidence Gap* (New York: Anchor Books, 1994); or Mary Pipher, *Reviving Ophelia: Saving the Selves of Adolescent Girls* (New York: Ballantine, 1994).

performance in math and science. Girls are more likely than boys to say they are not smart enough to achieve their dreams. Although both boys and girls experience a drop in self-esteem in early adolescence, the decline for girls is more severe, and it never catches up.

Peggy Orenstein reflects on the troubling results of this study in her book *Schoolgirls*:

> The results confirmed something that many women already knew too well. For a girl, the passage into adolescence is not just marked by menarche or a few new curves. It is marked by a loss of confidence in herself and her abilities, especially in math and science. It is marked by a scathingly critical attitude toward her body and a blossoming sense of personal inadequacy.[2]

Why is this passage into adolescence such a traumatic one for girls? Consider the following AAUW report findings:

- Boys are five times as likely to receive the teacher's attention and twelve times as likely to speak in class than girls.

- Boys receive more classroom attention, are called on more often and asked more complex questions than girls.

- Boys are more likely to be affirmed for their academic work, whereas girls are more likely to be affirmed for their behavior or clothing. The reverse is also true: boys are more likely to be criticized for their behavior, whereas girls are criticized for their academic work.

Several years have passed since the AAUW study was conducted, and many of my female undergraduate students tell me their school experiences were quite different than those reported. Yet in the student satisfaction inventories we conduct at the university where I teach, our female students consistently rate themselves less confidently than their male counterparts in their academic abilities, even though our female students consistently maintain higher grade point averages.

---

[2]Orenstein, *Schoolgirls*, p. xvi.

In addition, consider the reading materials given to boys and girls:

- 85 percent of all illustrations in textbooks are of boys.
- Three times as many stories that boys and girls read in school feature a boy as the main character rather than a female lead character.
- Students read six times as many male biographies than female biographies.

We learn during girlhood that our value lies not in our ability to think, reason and make informed decisions. Like the girls in the study who were affirmed for their clothing and good behavior, we learn that our value lies in our appearance and ability to please others.

Many recent books, such as Mary Pipher's *Reviving Ophelia*, have chronicled this painful passage in girls' lives, in which IQ scores drop, confident and energetic personalities become self-demeaning and self-critical, and optimism and curiosity turn to fear and depression. Pipher suggests that, as children, girls are valued for any number of things; however, when they enter adolescence, their acceptance and value is found primarily in appearance and popularity.

When I reflect on my adolescence, some of my most vivid memories have to do with this emphasis on appearance and popularity. When I was in seventh grade, I was going to have my first boy-girl party for my thirteenth birthday. We had the basement decorated, the snacks bought and the cake made. Then my trauma began: the day before my party I found out that another girl was having a party the same night. This other girl was very popular, and as friends began telling me they were not going to be able to come to my party, I feared the worst. And the worst happened. Six o'clock came and went. Eventually, one girl from school and a couple friends from church arrived. The saddest part was that I found myself wishing that the girl from school had not come at all. Why? Because I knew my classmates would find out about my failed party. If she had not come, maybe I could have pretended. Pipher suggests that girls do this kind of "pretending" all the time because of restricted opportunities for social rewards:

Girls become "female impersonators" who fit their whole selves into small, crowded spaces. Vibrant, confident girls become shy, doubting young women. Girls stop thinking, "Who am I? What do I want?" and start thinking, "What must I do to please others?"[3]

Lily, the fourteen-year-old heroine of the novel *The Secret Life of Bees* puts it this way: "I worried so much about how I looked and whether I was doing things right, I felt half the time I was impersonating a girl instead of really being one."[4] In adolescence, girls' authentic selves and voices are often silenced in an attempt to please others and live up to cultural expectations for girls and women.

BECOMING HEROINES IN OUR OWN LIVES

As adult women, we are on the other side of adolescence. Where exactly does that leave us? If we learned as girls, for example, that males are generally the heroes of textbooks, stories and classroom discussions, it can be a challenge to recover from that and learn to be heroines in our own lives. After learning to restrict ourselves and become "female impersonators" in order to please others and gain acceptance in adolescence, those pleasing and restricting tendencies do not magically disappear in adulthood. Pipher responds to this dilemma with sadness:

> Without some help, the loss of wholeness, self-confidence and self-direction can last well into adulthood. Many adult clients struggle with the same issues that overwhelmed them as adolescent girls. . . . Even sadder are the women who are not struggling, who have forgotten that they have selves worth defending.[5]

Rather than becoming a critic of the culture that has taught us so many damaging messages about our selfhood, many of us continue to quiet our authentic selves. We do not acknowledge or embrace the gift

---

[3]Pipher, *Reviving Ophelia*, p. 22.
[4]Sue Monk Kidd, *The Secret Life of Bees* (New York: Penguin, 2002), p. 9.
[5]Pipher, *Reviving Ophelia,* p. 25.

of the unique self God has created each of us to be, which is part of the image of God in us. When we silence our voices in this way, we limit our ability to have real relationships.

Contrary to the negative cultural messages we receive about our minds beginning in girlhood, the real truth, God's truth, is that we have been made thoughtful creatures. As women made in God's image and redeemed by Christ's love, this is who we are: rational beings-in-relationship with the ability to think, make predictions about the future, solve problems, make decisions, lovingly speak the truth and distinguish right from wrong. Our minds are gifts from God. Some of us have underestimated or neglected our minds, perhaps because of the discouraging messages we picked up from our parents, teachers, peers or other cultural influences. Others of us may have focused on our minds, perhaps even overemphasizing the importance of our intellect. Some of us may have intentionally worked to defy cultural stereotypes about women, but we may not have received much support or affirmation from the men and women around us in the process.

Jesus is the perfect image of God, and in him we find a model for how we can reflect God best through our minds and voices. God has created us for a unity and harmony of self in which we neither ignore nor overemphasize our minds (or any other part of ourselves). In other words, God wants whole women, not headless bodies or bodiless heads. In Christ we see a person who knows himself and uses his voice to build authentic relationships and to speak truth, even when it makes other people (such as the Pharisees) uncomfortable. Likewise, our minds are part of the image of God in us, whether we use them or not. The question, therefore, is *how* we use our minds. Following Christ's example, we can use our voices to lovingly speak truth and build authentic relationships.

USING YOUR VOICE

In order to effectively mirror God with your whole self, you must find and use your authentic voice. In her book *Growing Strong Daughters*, Lisa McMinn suggests that females, created in God's image, can reflect God in unique and distinct ways. However, "without voice," she argues, "these aspects of the image of God cannot be fully utilized."[6]

When psychologists talk about how some females lose their "voice" in adolescence, we are not referring to vocal chords. Rather, losing your voice means losing the freedom to be yourself. Reflect for a moment on what you were like before you hit the teenage years. Many of us felt free to say what we thought without filters. The filters we learn and apply in adolescence are inhibitors; they are messages we send ourselves that keep us from speaking our true thoughts. They may sound something like this:

- *Will she be angry if I say this?*
- *Will he still like me if I tell him what I really think?*
- *Just keep it to yourself, because nobody really cares.*
- *I wish she would stop saying that, but I don't want to sound mean or whiny.*

Of course, there is a difference between filters and good judgment. Filters inhibit our genuine voice, whereas good judgment helps us edit our thoughts so we do not impulsively blurt out the first things that come into our minds. Good judgment allows us to be respectful and sensitive, to think through what we want to say so we are able to share our real self with others. Filters, on the other hand, keep us from being real. For example, filters prevent many women from stating their opinions clearly and directly.

Reflect for a moment on the last group discussion you participated in with both men and women. How did the women speak in comparison to the men? Were the women more likely to make disclaimers before they spoke, such as, "I could be wrong, but . . ." or "This is only my opinion, but . . ."? If you notice a difference in how men and women speak in groups, it is not because we have different "communication genes." Rather, we grow up in a particular culture in which different kinds of behaviors are valued and reinforced more for males than for females. We

---

[6]Lisa Graham McMinn, *Growing Strong Daughters: Encouraging Girls to Become All They're Meant to Be* (Grand Rapids: Baker Books, 2000), p. 109.

learn in girlhood that to be accepted, we must tread lightly: be smart, but not smarter than boys; be strong, but not bossy; be kind, feminine and polite, but be yourself.

To find your voice is to embrace your unique selfhood. The woman who desires to use her authentic voice asks herself, *Who has God created me to be, and who is God calling me to become?* A life in which you reflect on who *you* are and who God is calling *you* to be is in contrast to an existence in which all of your life is lived for other people, without awareness of your own self. That kind of existence is all too common among women. Pipher writes, "Women often know how everyone in their family thinks and feels except themselves. They are great at balancing the needs of their co-workers, husbands, children and friends, but they forget to put themselves into the equation."[7] Not only is this kind of approach common, it is also rewarded and praised.

We will be much more effective and genuine in our relationships, our service and our care for others when we serve them from a place of authenticity. Consider the case of Mary, a forty-six-year-old woman whose husband's sexual infidelities have been a source of pain and marital tension for many years. Recently Mary joined a support group for wives of sex addicts. In the group she met Janie, and one week she and Janie went out for dessert after the group. Mary wanted to hear Janie's story, but she wasn't sure how to ask personal questions. Mary felt self-conscious and embarrassed about sharing her own story, so she made small talk instead. They waited over forty-five minutes for their desserts, and the server brought Mary regular coffee instead of decaf. Even though Mary gets headaches from caffeine, she didn't say anything so as not to bother anyone. At one point, Janie brought up a theological viewpoint that Mary disagreed with, but Mary just nodded and smiled, afraid to share her own thoughts about it. Janie also complimented Mary on a comment she had made in their last group meeting, but Mary was unsure how to either receive the compliment or return it. As they said goodbye, Mary

---

[7]Pipher, *Reviving Ophelia*, p. 25.

hoped they might make plans to get together again, but she wasn't sure if Janie had enjoyed her time and she wasn't sure how to ask, so she kept silent. She ended up going home and feeling disappointed in herself and the evening. Instead of sharing her real self and using her true voice with Janie, Mary presented a partial image of herself, restricting and quieting other important elements of her selfhood.

Reflect for a moment on your own life. Does Mary's situation sound familiar? Do you tend to quiet and restrict yourself in order not to step on anyone's toes, make them or you uncomfortable, or cause any tension? Ask yourself the following questions to assess how adept you are at using your voice:

- Am I comfortable expressing my opinion in a one-on-one situation, even if the other person thinks differently than me?

- Am I able to tell someone I have enjoyed talking with him or her?

- Am I able to say no to small requests, such as a friend asking me to drop off his or her child at my house for a few hours?

- Am I able to say no to requests for significant help if the requests seem unreasonable or if I have neither time nor ability to satisfy the requests?

- Am I able to tell a close friend or family member that he or she has hurt or upset me?

- Do I apologize when appropriate, but not over apologize, especially for things outside my control or responsibility?

- If I bought something I didn't like at a restaurant or a store, am I comfortable returning it or sending it back?

- Do I agree with people when my true feelings align with what they've said, or do I seem to agree with them even when I really disagree?

- Am I comfortable sharing my thoughts in a group setting?

- Am I able to ask a teacher, boss or friend for help?

- Do I feel comfortable making individual choices, or do I tend toward doing things I don't necessarily want to do in order to keep people from disliking me?

If you answered no to many of these questions, using your voice is probably a struggle. Sharing your opinions honestly, asking for or receiving help, and saying no when you need to are all elements of using your voice.

Take a moment to review the quotation at the opening of this chapter. Jane Austen's Anne is a wonderful example of a woman who has found and is able to use her true voice. She shares her opinions honestly and respectfully, even though they contradict those of her conversation partner, an older and respectable man. She does not apologize for or discredit her thoughts, but expresses them directly. Consequently, Captain Harville is able to interact not with a "female impersonator," but with a real woman.

We give ourselves and others a gift when we use our true voice. The beauty of using our voices is not that through learning to speak assertively we *get* what we *want* from people. Rather, by using our true voices, we *give* who we *are* to those around us. In a group I was facilitating recently, one of the members turned to a woman, Kelly, in the group who was exceedingly quiet and rarely shared her thoughts and opinions. "When I leave here," he told her, "I find myself wondering what you are thinking and feeling as you sit there so quietly. I would really like to know what you think about things." This comment was encouraging to Kelly, and she began opening up more in our meetings. After one session in which she spoke tearfully about her fears of being hurt in relationships and wanting to protect herself, I felt like I had met Kelly for the first time. When she shared her authentic self, she gave the group a gift—the gift of her true self.

As we begin to express our real thoughts and to ask for our needs to be met directly rather than indirectly, we allow people to interact with our real selves, not just shadows of who we think we should be. Of course, changing patterns is difficult, and others may not always respond as we might hope. Others may expect and want us to stay as we are, because it is familiar and comfortable. Beginning to use our voices can be frightening when it is a significant departure from our typical ways of being in relationship. Having someone in our corner who is supportive of this change is vital. With that support we can begin allowing people to see who we are and who we are becoming—a whole person made in God's image with unique thoughts, feelings and ideas.

TOOLS FOR THE JOURNEY

Build on small successes. If you resonated with Mary's situation and find it difficult to speak up and use your voice, the best solution is to *do something different.* Practice using your voice! Start small by making a list of safe ways to speak your mind. You might practice making simple requests. For example, you could ask a telemarketer to remove your name from the company's calling list. You might ask a cashier in a store to give you change without buying anything. As you get more comfortable doing these things, you might order a Coke in a restaurant, and then ask the server to switch you to iced tea for your refill.

In addition to making small requests, practice speaking up and sharing your real thoughts. For example, you could offer your opinion in your work meeting or small group, rather than remain silent until someone calls on you directly. Instead of saying, "I don't care," when your girlfriend asks you where you would like to meet for dinner, make a suggestion. You might ask a woman from your church or neighborhood whom you would like to know better if she would like to meet for coffee. You could tell a supportive coworker or friend that you appreciate his or her kindness.

As you construct your list of ways to practice making requests and sharing your thoughts, start with the easiest items. Monitor how you feel as you do these things. Is it as bad as you expected? Are you able to manage the discomfort? Did you get through it and survive? After completing an item on your list, reflect on the benefits of being able to share your thoughts, make requests and have them met. Also, try not to negate or minimize the importance of being able to do these things. Do not underestimate the importance of small successes. Each victory is a building block toward change. The same skills that allow you to be successful with those items at the beginning of your list will allow you to be successful with the more challenging items near the end of your list.

Practice saying no. Are you seemingly unable to say no? Mary was so accommodating and such a servant that she told me she sometimes felt like she was wearing a sign that said, "Yes—whatever the question—I'll do it." Others of you may be just the opposite. You may say no to just about everything, unwilling to give of yourself. This is a whole different issue and one that will be addressed more fully in chapter eight. If, however, you are a yes-sayer, then this tool for the journey is meant for you.

Part of using your voice is speaking truth to people. When friends, family members, coworkers or church members ask you to do something, sometimes the truthful answer is no. However, yes-women struggle to even say that word. When a request is made of you, you aren't sure what to do or how to respond, so you end up saying yes. You may be afraid that if you say no, people will think you are mean or ungodly. Consequently, you get burnt out, exhausted and sometimes even resentful. You overextend yourself and are unable to devote as much time or energy to the most important things in your life—your relationships. To use your true voice is to do an honest assessment of requests and to provide others with honest answers.

Begin to monitor yourself. Are you unable to refuse requests, even when they are unreasonable or outside your ability? If you are a yes-woman, the next time someone asks you to do something, thoughtfully evaluate the request before you respond. You might tell the other party you will get back to him or her so that you can assess the situation and honestly determine your ability to fulfill the request. First, consider the request itself. Is it manageable and reasonable? Don't be afraid to contact the other party and ask for additional information. If someone asks you to coordinate the neighborhood garage sale, what exactly does that mean? Will you just be doing the advertising and setting up signs, or will you be in charge of every aspect of the event? In order to give an honest answer, you need to first understand what is being asked of you.

If the request is more than you are able or willing to do at that time, tell the other party by first *restating* the request. This assures the other person that you understand the nature of the request and have thought about it. Then, *briefly* explain why you cannot or will not be able to fulfill the request. Finally, actually *say no*. For example, "I understand you would like me to coordinate the community garage sale, but I have out-of-town family coming to stay with me that weekend. I will be unable to take care of all the details or attend the sale because of my guests, so no, I cannot do it." It is important to remember, however, that you do not have to give people a reason for saying no. Too often, I see women who say yes all the time because their only reason for saying no is that they did not want to do the request or because they had nothing planned during that time. If you are asked to do something and do not want to do it, that is okay. While service is important, it is also important to care for yourself and respect your own needs and feelings. Each of us differs on whether we tend to be yes-sayers or no-sayers. If you lean toward being a yes-sayer, then practicing saying no is important for you. On the other hand, if you tend to be a no-sayer, then the area in which you probably need to grow is in learning to say yes!

It might be helpful to keep a few additional things in mind as you begin practicing your "no" muscle. When you respond negatively to someone's request, try to do it quickly. You do not need to explain six different ways why you cannot or will not manage the garage sale. Try not to over-apologize or begin offering other services for the person in order to assuage your guilt. If you cannot do it or don't want to, it is okay to say no! You do not need to babysit your neighbor's children for the next three months to "make up" for saying no.

I am not suggesting that you begin saying no to everything. We honor God by giving of ourselves to help others. We cannot, however, say yes all the time without some things suffering, like our family relationships, our physical health or our intimacy with God. We must be discerning about which things in our lives should come first. In order to honor priorities, we must sometimes say no to things. By learning to distinguish which activities we can and should decline, and then respectfully providing others with an honest answer, we honor God with our minds and our voices.

Use your voice to communicate directly, rather than indirectly. After you begin to feel more comfortable using your voice to ask for small requests, share your thoughts and say no when necessary, identify some of the more serious scenarios in which you find it difficult to use your voice. Is it horrific to think about telling a friend that he or she has hurt you, even though you are becoming bitter and resentful? In order to practice using your voice, prepare for the conversation ahead of time. Decide when and where you hope to talk with your friend. Imagine the scene in your mind. Close your eyes and picture yourself in the room. As you create that vivid scene, imagine the message you will give your friend.

When giving this kind of feedback, it is helpful to include several elements in your message. First, *express* your feelings in an emotionally neutral manner by using an I-message. When we begin statements with words like, "You are so mean," we sound as though we're attacking. Naturally, people become defensive when we are on the offensive. On the other hand, if you focus on yourself and your own feelings, you are more likely to defuse the other person. You are, after all, the final authority on your feelings. An I-message, however, does not just mean adding an "I feel like . . ." to the beginning of any sentence. For example, saying, "I feel like you are a jerk" reflects an opinion rather than an emotion. An attacking statement like this is also not likely to open the doors of communication! Rather, when you use an I-message, name *your* specific feeling, such as, "I felt lonely . . . or angry . . . or sad . . . or scared." It is helpful to remain calm, because if you are crying profusely, this can come across as manipulative or passive-aggressive to the listener. If you sound angry while you are saying you feel hurt, this is also confusing. Even while discussing painful emotions, it is helpful if you are able to step back and talk about your feelings in a calm and clear manner.

After you have shared your feelings with an I-message, describe the *specific behavior* that upset you. Make sure you focus on the behavior, not the person. It's also helpful to be as concise and clear as possible. Avoid words like *always* or *never*, because there is always an exception to "always" or "never." Therefore, in order to be heard, briefly state what hurt you. For example, you might say "I felt hurt when you made that joke about my taste in clothes in front of your other friends." This message is more specific and less threatening than if you said something like, "You are spiteful and vindictive," or "You are always mocking me in front of other people."

Once you have clearly and succinctly described the hurtful behavior, you should then clarify what you want from the situation. Directly *request* what you need for things to be better. Try not to undermine your message with profuse apologies or disclaimers. Instead, conclude your message with a concise statement of what you would like from your friend, such as, "I wish you wouldn't joke like that in front of people I don't know well." After sharing your feelings and your request, give your friend a chance to respond. Finally, thank the other person for listening to your feedback and talking with you about it.

When we are angry or maltreated and remain silent, we typically still communicate those feelings. We may just communicate them indirectly, through not calling our friend, being short when we speak to him or her, or withholding intimate information we would normally share. By speaking honestly, we live out of our wholeness and invite others to do the same.

Even though it may be uncomfortable to do this, consider the motive and intent behind your message. When you give direct feedback to a friend, you are essentially telling the other person, "You are a good friend, and I care about you. I feel like there is something between us, and we're both afraid to mention it. Instead of staying silent, let's talk about what has come between us so we can deal with it. I value our friendship, and I want things to be better."

When we communicate with people directly, by making requests, sharing our thoughts, saying no or giving feedback, we speak truth from our hearts. We also give others a chance to interact with the real us when we speak honestly in these ways. If we say no to a friend, he or she gets to talk with the person who is genuinely overwhelmed with current responsibilities, rather than a woman pretending she can always handle one more thing. If we give feedback to a friend, that friend is able to see a woman who is genuinely hurt, rather than one offering polite but insincere laughter. Jesus used his voice to speak truth and build relationships. When we choose to speak honestly, we follow Christ's model and grow in our ability to reflect God to the world around us.

4

Negative Self-Talk

HOW THE WAY WE THINK
AFFECTS THE WAY WE FEEL

I know what you tell yourself, you tell yourself . . .

Who told you that nothing about you is alright?

It's just no use, it's just no good, you'll never be okay . . .

You tell you yourself that you're not pretty . . .

Tell yourself that no one sees Plain Jane . . .

Tell yourself there's nothing worse than the pain inside and the way it hurts . . .

NATALIE MERCHANT
"TELL YOURSELF," *MOTHERLAND*

◦⟨⟩◦

*I*n order for us to use our voices, we must first listen to our voices. For many of us, however, when we listen to our inner thoughts, we don't hear our authentic selves. Like the girl in Natalie Merchant's song, we hear the critical things we tell ourselves. Psychologists refer to this critical voice as negative self-talk. It is the voice inside our heads commenting on our words and actions throughout the day. It is not an external voice, but our own self-reflective thoughts. Those thoughts may sometimes seem like a broken record, replaying over and over again.

Julie, a twenty-four-year-old single woman I saw in counseling for depression and low self-esteem, experienced this kind of repetitive, negative self-talk. When I asked her to chronicle her inner dialogue, she discovered that throughout the day her self-talk was filled with negative comments, such as:

- *That was so stupid, you're such a failure.*
- *You'll never make it, so don't even try.*
- *Be quiet, you sound like an idiot.*
- *You can't wear that—you're too fat.*

Julie was surprised at the harsh nature of her self-talk after completing this exercise. Reflect for a moment on the things you tell yourself. Is your self-talk critical and demeaning? Is your inner dialogue harsh and ungracious, perhaps filled with words you wouldn't speak to an enemy, much less a friend?

Self-talk is powerful. We hear the words of that voice more than any other voice in our lives. If our self-talk sounds like a critical, negative tape that continuously runs, it can be difficult to speak with confidence or self-assurance. Negative self-talk can block us from hearing the still, small voice of God speaking to us. Words have power, and if we speak self-rejecting words to ourselves, we fail to acknowledge our true identity as beloved children of God.

Negative self-talk is problematic because of its damaging effects on our self-esteem and confidence, and because it is so often inaccurate and unrealistic. Negative self-talk is not exclusive to a particular gender or stage in life. Rather, men and women, young and old, struggle with it. When our self-talk is negative and critical, it often contains thinking patterns that keep us from accurately seeing ourselves and others as whole persons created in God's image. Psychologists sometimes refer to these cognitive roadblocks as irrational thoughts or cognitive distortions.[1] In this chapter, I will review several thought patterns that often block our

---

[1] See David Burns, *Feeling Good: The New Mood Therapy* (New York: Avon Books, 1980) for a thorough examination of cognitive distortions.

paths to hearing and using our true voices, as well as suggestions for overcoming those roadblocks. We can grow in our ability to image God as we begin to see ourselves and others as who we really are and who we are becoming through Christ's redemptive work.

ROADBLOCK #1: IT'S ALL OR NOTHING

"She's just a bad friend," Julie told me after a friend hurt her feelings with an insensitive comment at a recent gathering. "Katie embarrassed me and hurt my feelings, and she's not a good friend." Although Katie was a close friend of Julie's and had never said anything like this before, this one incident had seemingly placed her on Julie's "bad friend" list. Instead of being upset with Katie's words or her hurtful actions in that one situation, Julie was upset at Katie's whole being (i.e., she *is* a bad friend, rather than she *did* a hurtful thing). Julie was engaging in the all-or-nothing thinking trap, seeing Katie as either all good or all bad.

The problem with this kind of thinking is that if I make one mistake, it's over. My whole sense of identity is shaken. Do you remember playing on the seesaw when you were a child? Although I loved it, I also tended to get a little sick to my stomach if I seesawed too long or had an overly rambunctious partner. This kind of thinking is like living life on the seesaw. One minute you're on the upswing, enjoying the cool breeze of perfection, praise and accomplishment. The next minute your rear end slams to the ground as you are overwhelmed by failure, a critical word, a mistake or a slip-up.

Living in the extremes of this kind of thinking is exhausting. We never feel constant in our perceptions of ourselves, because whether we are good or bad depends on temporal circumstances, performances and feedback. We also never feel constant in our perception of others, because whether they are good or bad depends on so many particulars. *Will he forget to kiss me goodbye? Will she remember to call me this week? Will he clean up his room?*

The root of this black-and-white thinking is often perfectionistic standards. *If you live up to my standards, then you are wonderful, but if you fail to meet those standards and disappoint me, then you* are *a disappointment.* Kathleen Fischer examines the impact of these perfectionistic tendencies in the mother-daughter relationship: "A woman's spiritual challenge is often that of letting go of images of perfect mothers and perfect daughters who fully meet each other's needs and expectations. This means learning to view our mothers with compassion."[2] Fischer is writing specifically about the mother-daughter relationship, but her words could apply to other relationships as well, such as when we carry unrealistic expectations of husbands, boyfriends, fathers, friends or siblings. When we increase our compassion and let go of expectations of perfection, we allow people to make mistakes. Since it is a guarantee that people will make mistakes, we are more realistic when we expect and accept this. In addition, it is likely that the same perfectionistic rules, or even worse, apply to how we think about and judge ourselves. Therefore, we also need to begin viewing ourselves with more compassion, accepting that we will make mistakes and can even learn and grow from those mistakes.

None of us is all bad or all good all the time. Some of us, for example, have been wounded by the men in our lives—perhaps we were sexually violated by a man, or maybe we had an absent father or an abusive uncle. In our desperate longing to feel safe and secure, we may try to protect ourselves through all-or-nothing thinking. Because we were hurt by one man (or perhaps many men), we may act as if all men are threatening or dangerous or bad. Although this may *feel* true, the reality is that this kind of extreme thinking is a lie. Not all men (or all women for that matter) are bad, and not all women (or men) are good. As we begin replacing the lies of extreme thinking with the truth of realistic thinking, we will be able to more accurately view ourselves and others with greater compassion, knowing we are all people made in God's image.

---

[2]Kathleen Fischer, *Women at the Well: Feminist Perspectives on Spiritual Direction* (New York: Paulist, 1988), p. 202.

ROADBLOCK #2: SHOULDING

Another maladaptive thinking pattern many women fall into is the "shoulding" trap, in which we live our lives according to a rigid set of rules we believe people should obey at all times. These rules are not national or religious laws. Instead, they are inflexible personal convictions about what one should or shouldn't do, say or feel in various situations. Frequently we do not think of these expectations consciously as a list of rules. Rather, we just assume these things are what people "should" do, and it often seems perfectly obvious to us. Therefore, we tend to get frustrated, angry or hurt when people fail to live up to these obvious standards. In addition, we feel guilty ourselves when we fall short. Sometimes we may even punish ourselves or others who fail to live up to that unconscious list of rules. We can identify our list of shoulds by examining situations in which we respond with thoughts or statements like, "You shouldn't have done that," "You ought to know better," or "You have to change."

Am I suggesting that having standards is problematic? Of course not. As Christians we are called to live godly lives with integrity. We worship a God who tells us to "be holy, because I am holy" (Leviticus 11:44). Throwing out behavioral standards is not the solution. However, our shoulds are not always biblical. As psychologist Bruce Narramore points out, "People often live under unbearable guilt because of their inability to measure up to the standards of parents, society, or a Christian subculture. Tragically, these standards frequently do not represent the voice of God at all!"[3] More often, these standards are cultural behaviors we learned from our families of origin. Because our families are all so different, our individual expectations differ as well. For example, you may have grown up in a home in which you learned that people should be on time, be responsible, get up early and not waste time. However, your husband may have learned that people should be relaxed and easygoing,

---

[3]Bruce Narramore, *No Condemdation: Rethinking Guilt Motivation in Counseling, Preaching & Parenting* (Grand Rapids: Academie Books, 1984), p. 301.

that they should enjoy life and enjoy people, and that it is the journey rather than the destination that is most important. Can you imagine the collision of these two lists of shoulds? Is one of you more "Christian" than the other in your standards? Certainly not—as one could argue for the Christian virtue in both of these Mary and Martha approaches to life.

When our lists of shoulds become rigid and inflexible, and when we are unable to see the value in other people's approaches to life, we fail to see and treat them as whole persons. In addition, when we punish ourselves for failing to live up to our own lists of shoulds, we often become paralyzed. When we fall into shoulding, our minds get clouded with guilty thoughts about how we *ought* to have a clean house all the time, or people *must* like us, or we *have* to be pleasant all the time. Guilt that produces change is wonderful, but usually guilt produces more guilt. Shoulding often causes unnecessary guilt. Feeling guilty for failing to meet unrealistic expectations usually produces little benefit, as we can't change our behavior to be *perfect* all the time so that people *always* like us, find us pleasant and find our houses perfectly arranged.

Take time to reflect on your own list of shoulds. What kinds of things are you punishing yourself and others for doing or not doing? Are your expectations for yourself and others realistic? In order to use your true voice, you must first listen to that voice. Perhaps it would be helpful to begin letting go of the list of what you *should* be in order to find and accept your true voice: "Our deepest calling is to grow into our own authentic selfhood," Parker Palmer writes, "whether or not it conforms to some image of who we *ought* to be."[4]

ROADBLOCK #3: I JUST KNOW (MIND-READING)

"It was awful," Julie told me after a date with Joe, a man she had been romantically interested in. "He thought I was fat and boring. I just wanted it to end." When asked how she discovered Joe's thoughts about

---

[4]Parker Palmer, *Let Your Life Speak: Listening for the Voice of Vocation* (San Francisco: Jossey-Bass, 2000), p. 16.

her, Julie replied, "I could just tell. It was obvious." Julie's assumption that she knew another person's inner thoughts is a good example of a thinking trap—mind-reading—that keeps us from seeing ourselves and others as whole persons.

When we attempt to engage in mind-reading, we come to conclusions about what other people are thinking and feeling and why they are acting in particular ways. If we get caught in this cognitive trap, we often think we are especially adept at discerning how people are thinking and feeling towards *us*. Even without Joe giving any verbal indications that he thought Julie was unattractive or poor company, she imagined those were his thoughts and feelings toward her.

Not only do we imagine other people's thoughts and feelings when we attempt to mind-read, we often act as if the person has said those things to us directly. Even though Joe never told Julie he thought she was fat or boring, she treated him as if he had done as much. Julie became defensive and even attacking in their conversation, not because of the *reality* of his opinion of her, but because of what she *believed* was his opinion of her.

Reflect for a moment on times you might do this. Did you just *know* that when you had that conversation with your husband last night, he was thinking that you are always late and irresponsible? Did you berate yourself after a conversation with your boss because you were sure he was thinking about how inarticulate and incompetent you are? Did you get angry with your daughter because you could just tell she made that comment to intentionally hurt you? Did you get hurt by another woman in your small group after she shifted around and looked at another member of the group when you were sharing, sure that those actions were a reflection of her negative feelings toward you? Do you find yourself reconstructing the inner thoughts or feelings of others after a conversation or party, imagining what they thought about the way you looked or the words you said?

Of course, it is natural to wonder about what people think of us to some degree. Sometimes, however, we come to conclusions about what others think without sound evidence. When we do this, we do not treat other people as whole persons. We treat them as we have imagined and created them to be in our minds, and we miss out on the reality of other people. For example, Julie interpreted Joe's dropped eyes and meager conversation as boredom and disdain, but perhaps he was nervous and scared himself. Rather than thinking about Julie's size or charisma, he may have been focused on his own bumbling speech and nervous movements. If so, Julie missed out on what could have been a meaningful relationship. Sometimes people are thinking negatively of us. But sometimes they are not. When we act as if we just *know,* we work against the development of authentic relationships.

ROADBLOCK #4: WHAT IF . . . ?

Another thinking trap we may engage in is the slippery slope of what psychologists call catastrophic thinking. We may see a potential problem and begin reviewing the endless series of worst-case scenarios: *What if the storm gets worse and we get into an accident on the way home? What if I never get married? What if my son gets injured in the game? What if my husband has an affair and leaves me? What if I can't have children? What if we can't pay these bills and lose everything? What if my daughter dates the wrong boy and ends up in a bad situation? What if my husband dies and I am left with nothing?*

Rather than deal with the reality of the current situation, we get lost in and distracted by our "what if" thoughts. Although we often believe this kind of thinking increases our control by preparing us for the worst, the reality is that it does just the opposite. It keeps us from living in the moment and working toward the solutions for real problems, and it increases what is often unnecessary anxiety.

Julie, for example, engaged in this kind of catastrophic thinking regarding her weight and future relationships. Julie was about seventy-five pounds overweight and would sometimes say, "What if I never lose weight? If I'm not thin, then I'll never find a good man and get married." Rather than motivate her, catastrophic thinking froze her. Making changes in health and eating habits requires focus on the present moment, for example, making healthy choices right *now* to work toward *future* goals. However, when Julie began catastrophizing she would get stuck in her fears about the future. These "what if" scenarios depressed her, making her feel more helpless to change and out of control. For Julie, food was a source of comfort and solace, so she would end up sabotaging her healthy eating in order to ease and silence her anxious thoughts about the future.

In addition, Julie's thoughts about her weight and marriage were unrealistic. She became anxious and depressed because of her fear that she would never marry if she wasn't thin. However, the reality is that many overweight people do marry, and marry happily. In addition, many thin people never marry, or have unhappy marriages. The relationship between weight and marriage is a loose one at best. Julie's catastrophic thinking caused her unnecessary anxiety and froze her from making changes she wanted to see in her life. This anxiety is rooted not in *reality,* but in her own catastrophic *fears* about reality.

ROADBLOCK #5: THE NEGATIVE FILTER

I love the smell of coffee brewing, and there is nothing quite like the taste of a fresh cup when I get up in the morning. Imagine if my husband offered me a cup one morning, but instead of pouring the coffee from the brewed pot, he pulled out the filter and dumped the grounds into my cup. I would be pretty upset! But sometimes we do this very thing in our thinking—holding onto the bitter, distasteful parts and throwing out the good stuff.

Julie came to see me one week after spending the weekend at her mother's house. She spent the first twenty minutes telling me in great detail how her mother had made a critical comment about her weight during breakfast one morning. Only upon inquiry did I learn that Julie and her mother also had several meaningful conversations in which her mother affirmed Julie's work accomplishments and personal growth. Julie's thinking pattern in this situation was like a mental filter. The negative events were like the coffee grounds my husband poured into my cup. Julie held on to these negative comments and thought about them again and again at length. The positive aspects of the weekend, however, were like the water that dripped through the filter. Although it was the best part, it was seemingly forgotten and thrown away. Julie filtered out the positive elements of the situation and remembered only the negative.

Women might engage in this kind of thinking in a variety of situations. After a telephone conversation with your husband, are you able to recall with perfect accuracy his sarcastic comment about your mother? But do you have trouble remembering the thoughtful questions or compliments he gave you? If you meet with your boss, do you remember the six positive contributions she affirmed you for, or are you focused on the two suggestions she offered to improve your performance? If you led a Bible study and thought it went well, but a friend mentioned that you spoke quickly, do you criticize yourself, focusing on your friend's single comment, or do you focus on the thanks offered by several of the women as they left the study?

When we remember only the negative aspects of conversations or interactions with other people, we do not treat them or ourselves as whole persons. We split our understandings of the people and the situations into either positive *or* negative, and then we go on to listen and value *only* the negative. In order to grow toward wholeness in ourselves, we need to learn to interpret the world and people around us in a more holistic manner. When we focus only on certain negative parts of situations, we fail to take in the whole picture. Consequently, we miss out on the best part. We complain about how bitter the coffee grounds taste, all while there's a full pot of warm coffee that has been forgotten or ignored.

OTHER ROADBLOCKS

I have presented five of the most common thinking roadblocks, but psychologists identify several other cognitive distortions. Ask yourself which thinking traps you fall into as you review this brief summary:

- *Emotional reasoning.* You assume that because you feel a certain way, that is reality. For example, *I feel incompetent, therefore I am incompetent,* or *I think he's embarrassed of me, so he is embarrassed of me.*

* *Fortune-telling.* In "what if" thinking, you *worry* about the future. In "fortune-telling," you think you *know* the future. You're convinced that your predictions that things will turn out badly are going to happen, and you act accordingly. *I know if I tried to go back to school, I would fail, so I won't go.*

* *Overgeneralization.* In the "negative filter," you remember only the bad stuff. In "overgeneralization," you take one single negative event and see it happening over and over again. For example, you might think, *I really messed up that interview and didn't get the job. It's hopeless because I'll never get a job.*

* *Magnification and minimization.* This is sometimes called the "binocular trick" because you magnify all your negative qualities and minimize all your good qualities. If you perform well, you shrug it off. If, however, you make a mistake, you exaggerate the importance of it. For example, *Being a good cook doesn't mean anything. Anyone can follow a recipe. I just wish I had gone to school and had a real career like my sister. I think my husband would respect me more, and we wouldn't have the problems we do now.*

* *Personalization.* You act as if everything people say or do is somehow about you. If you are in a social setting and someone gets upset or leaves the room, it must be a reaction to you personally. *He made that comment in the meeting right after I spoke. He's trying to show me up and show the boss he's smarter.*

In "Tell Yourself," Natalie Merchant sings about the messages girls tell themselves. " 'It's such a tough world,' that's what you say. Well I know, I know it's easier said than done, but that's enough, girl. Give it away."[5] When we think in fragmented ways, we keep ourselves from hearing our true voices and from seeing ourselves and others as whole persons.

---

[5]Natalie Merchant, "Tell Yourself," *Motherland,* Elektra Entertainment, 2001. Lyrics written by Natalie Merchant ©2001 Indian Love Bride Music.

Therefore, we need to begin identifying and restructuring those destructive thought patterns. Through our union with Christ, we are to renew our minds (Ephesians 4:23). Like all change, this is easier said than done, but in order to begin listening to our authentic voices, we must learn to let go of our distorted thinking patterns.

TOOLS FOR THE JOURNEY

Practice thought-stopping. If negative self-talk is hindering you in your desire to use your true voice, the first step is *attending* to that inner voice. You have probably heard people yell in the heat of an argument, "I don't have to listen to this!" While I'm not suggesting that you begin yelling at yourself, you can borrow the sentiment. Begin recording over that negative, critical tape by speaking truth to yourself: you *don't* have to listen to negative self-talk.

When I counseled Julie, I asked her to try an experiment to monitor her negative self-talk. Julie often wore her hair in a ponytail, and I suggested that she wear one of her rubber hair bands around her wrist for a week. Every time she caught herself tuning in to that negative tape, she was to snap the band and say *Stop!* to herself. Now, if you decide to try this, I'll give you the same warning I gave Julie: I'm not suggesting that you punish yourself with the rubber band (for example, holding it back five or six inches and letting it rip). This is not an exercise in self-flagellation. Rather, use the band as a physical reminder to stop what you're doing.

Your critical self-talk will not magically disappear with this thought-stopping technique, but you will become more aware of your critical voice. You may be surprised at how much just *noticing* something can lead to positive changes in your ability to reflect God in your inner voice more and more.

Challenge your thinking. As you monitor your self-talk, you may find that you get caught in a number of cognitive roadblocks. For example, perhaps you engage in all-or-nothing thinking quite a bit. Learning to identify and name this thinking trap is huge progress. When you catch yourself in the act of all-or-nothing thinking, begin to gently challenge and reframe your thoughts.

For example, after discussing Julie's interaction with the girlfriend who had hurt her feelings, we developed a challenge list. On this list, I asked her to reflect on a variety of questions, such as What percent of the time is Katie a bad friend? Is it 100 percent of the time? If not, then when has she *not* been a bad friend? What are some things Katie has done since you have known her that weren't so bad? What are some not-so-bad things Katie has done even this month? What is one objectively nice or good thing about Katie?

When Julie attempted to mind-read with Joe, we developed a different kind of challenge list. After discussing her beliefs about Joe's thoughts, I asked Julie to describe her evidence for those beliefs. Julie mentioned his apparent discomfort and averted gaze while speaking to her. I then asked her to add these questions to her challenge list: What is another way to interpret this? For example, how else could we look at Joe's gaze and movements? Is there any other explanation for his behavior?

When Julie began catastrophizing about her weight and fears about not getting married, I asked her to incorporate additional questions to her challenge list: What would be the worst thing that could happen? Was it really that she wouldn't get married? In contrast, what would be the best thing that could happen? I then worked with Julie on exploring what would *probably* happen in the situation, based on what she knew about other people's marriages, their weights and her own relationship history.

If you notice yourself getting stuck in one of these cognitive roadblocks, stop yourself in the act. Then, challenge yourself and evaluate the accuracy of that thought. Are you seeing yourself, others or the world around you in a whole way, or are you splitting them into parts and ignoring certain aspects? Are you interpreting the situation in a limited way? A good way to coach yourself through challenging your thoughts is to imagine that you are sitting with your best friend. If your best friend was sharing these same thoughts with you, what would you say to her?

Begin listening to that voice, and perhaps you can begin treating *yourself* as a friend.

Incorporate new thinking. It is not enough to just stop or challenge our negative or irrational thoughts; we must go one step further. In order to begin thinking in a more holistic manner, we need to replace those negative, irrational, fragmented thoughts with more accurate thoughts that incorporate a holistic view of ourselves, others and the world around us. These replacement thoughts should be filled with truth about who we are and who we are becoming in Christ.

I am not talking about filling your mind with ungrounded affirmations just for the sake of affirmations. Rather, I am suggesting that you "take captive every thought to make it obedient to Christ" (2 Corinthians 10:5). Replace those negative, inaccurate thoughts with the truth of God about your real identity as one created in his image who belongs to God. Begin incorporating new thinking that better allows you to see yourself and others as whole persons. You might even write out some of these truths on index cards to post on your bathroom mirror or dashboard as a reminder of who you are and who you are becoming in Christ. Some things you might include on your truth cards are:

- *I am a child of God and deserve love and respect.*
- *Regardless of what happens in this situation, I will be okay. God will not leave me or forsake me.*
- *Other people will make mistakes and disappoint me, and it will be okay. We'll get through it.*
- *I have God-given intelligence, and I am called to use it.*
- *I have worth and value. I am a woman made in God's image.*
- *I cannot control the future.*
- *My true voice is given to me by God, and it is one worth hearing.*
- *I am growing. Christ is renewing me and making me whole.*
- *It's okay to make mistakes. I can even learn from them. It's through my weaknesses that Christ is made strong.*

- *It's okay to ask for and receive help from others.*
- *I am not responsible for making other people feel happy or successful or okay. In fact, I cannot make other people feel these ways.*
- *I am learning to show my true self, the unique woman God created me to be, to others.*
- *This painful or difficult feeling or situation will pass. I will get through it.*
- *I am not perfect, and I am not a failure. I am a mix of good and bad, and I am growing and learning every day.*

Reflect on the truths in Scripture and the reality of God's love for you. Just because you *feel* unloved or unlovable does not mean you *are* unloved or unlovable. That is emotional reasoning! Remind yourself of the objective reality of how intensely loved you are: "Neither death nor life, neither angels nor demons, neither the present nor the future, nor any powers, neither height nor depth, nor anything else in all creation, will be able to separate us from the love of God that is in Christ Jesus our Lord" (Romans 8:38-40). If you are overwhelmed by the sin in your life and feel like you must be beyond Christ's reach, remember that Jesus "gave himself for us to redeem us from *all* wickedness" (Titus 2:14, italics mine). Jesus didn't die for *some* of your sins. There is nothing you can do that is outside God's reach. When you replace your negative and inaccurate thoughts with the truth of God's Word, you are more able to participate in and experience the wholeness Christ offers.

The psalmist sings, "May these words of my mouth and this meditation of my heart / be pleasing in your sight, / LORD, my Rock and my Redeemer" (Psalm 19:14). You have been made a thoughtful person with the ability to make decisions, develop opinions and speak your voice. This is one of the gifts God has given you as a child made in his own image. When you challenge the thoughts that keep you from seeing yourself and others as the whole people God intends us to be and become, you please your Creator with the meditations of your heart. By using your mind, your thoughts and your voice, you reveal the gift God has given, and you grow in your ability to reflect and mirror God to the world around you.

5

When Your Emotions Get the Best of You

GROWING THROUGH
ANGER, ANXIETY AND DEPRESSION

Come to me, all you who are weary and burdened, and I will give you rest.

Take my yoke upon you and learn from me, for I am gentle

and humble in heart, and you will find rest for your souls.

For my yoke is easy and my burden is light.

JESUS CHRIST
MATTHEW 11:28-30

When my husband and I decided we were ready to have children, I began reading every book I could find on fertility and pregnancy, fearing we might encounter difficulties conceiving. We were, of course, overjoyed when we found out I was pregnant. Unfortunately, our excitement was short-lived. After a ten-hour drive to surprise my husband's parents with our news, we walked back in the door to our house and my stomach dropped. I had been having mild cramps much of the way home and had felt something unmistakable as I stood up—something I desperately did not want to feel. I ran to the bathroom immediately, and when my husband came in with our bags he found me in tears. After several confusing doctor visits and ultrasounds, our loss was confirmed a few weeks later.

Even though I had read in all my pregnancy books how common miscarriages are, I was still overwhelmed by sadness and grief. Although some people did not understand my feelings, I loved that baby already. Even as I'm writing these words now, when so much time has passed and I have a healthy little boy sleeping upstairs, my eyes are filled with tears. The sadness was unlike any I had known before. I couldn't explain it, and it didn't completely make sense to me. But it was there, and I couldn't will it away. Good people reminded me that miscarriages are often the body's way of taking care of a deformed fetus and that it was probably a blessing in the long run. I understood these words, and intellectually they made sense to me. But I'll be honest: it didn't feel like a blessing.

Not only was I overcome by sadness, but anxiety and worry about my ability to have children reached a new level. Just having a miscarriage increased my fears, and when my doctor diagnosed a uterine abnormality, that worry escalated even more. Well-meaning people kept telling me that my next pregnancy would be fine, but I had just lost a baby and knew the truth: there were no guarantees. I knew that was a promise they couldn't make. What if I couldn't get pregnant again? What if my body was unable to carry a pregnancy to term?

In addition to my sadness and worry, it seemed that everywhere I looked there were unfit parents. That sounds awful and judgmental, which is exactly how I felt. Young expectant moms who were still kids themselves were in every grocery store with their beautiful pregnant bellies. Parents inappropriately screaming at their kids were seemingly always in line directly in front of me at Wal-Mart. I couldn't escape the unfairness of it all. My husband and I were married; we were ready; we were passionately devoted to raising a child to love Jesus. And here we were—childless.

Although my story of feeling overwhelmed by sadness, worry and anger involved a loss, your story may be altogether different. Your world might be falling apart in a million different ways—from a failed marriage to financial distress to hurtful relationships. Perhaps you too have lost someone or something that was precious to you. Maybe your husband or boyfriend has betrayed you, your mother or father has disappointed you, your colleague or boss has insulted you, or perhaps you have been undone by the pain of rejection from a trusted friend. In an effort to drown your pain, you may have sought escape through alcohol or sex or work or food, and now you are weighed down by guilt and shame as well. On the other hand, you may be overwhelmed by feelings of sadness, worry or anger, and you do not know why. You *wish* you had a story with a particular event or person or situation that caused you to feel this pain. You feel lost in these emotions, and you wonder how you can find your way out when you are unsure how you got there in the first place.

In this chapter, I will explore how we can grow in wholeness when bombarded by painful emotions like anger, worry and depression. Of course, painful emotions affect all of us, male and female, but I will focus on how women experience emotions. I will also examine the importance of allowing ourselves to experience emotions, viewing them as signals or messages, and finding hope and growth amidst pain and despair. I will also consider when to seek the help of a professional counselor, pastor or physician.

GET REAL WITH YOUR EMOTIONS

In the bestseller *Divine Secrets of the Ya-Ya Sisterhood,* the main character describes her mother's emotions: "Mama did not think; Mama just felt."[1] The mother struggled with a psychiatric disorder, but the statement reflects a common female stereotype—women are emotional, not rational. Perhaps because of this negative stereotype of the irrational and overly emotional nature of females, many women have learned to silence their feelings. Certain emotions, like anger, are particularly taboo. Kathleen

---

[1]Rebecca Wells, *Divine Secrets of the Ya-Ya Sisterhood* (New York: HarperCollins, 1996), p. 112.

Fisher reflects on this bias against the acknowledgment or expression of negative emotions in women:

> The image of the ideal or good woman extols patience, kindness, and caring; anger is out of place in such an image. People speak disparagingly of "angry women." Anger in women threatens others, and so is labeled unfeminine, immature, even hysterical. These taboos against women's direct expression of anger make it easier to turn the anger inward rather than risk disapproval and the loss of important relationships.[2]

In our God-given longing to nurture relationships, we may suppress certain emotions. Because we are unsure how to cope with these painful emotions, we may pretend we do not experience them. Or worse yet, we may be *unable* to feel them.

Annie, a thirty-five-year-old woman I saw in counseling after her husband had been unfaithful to her, was unable to experience anger. "I'm not sure why, and maybe I should feel angry at him," she told me, "but I just don't." Here was a woman with every reason to be mad, and the reality was, she did feel angry. Unfortunately, she had turned that anger inward and was attacking herself on every front for her husband's unfaithfulness. The problem with this response, aside from the resulting depression, is that Annie's anger could have been a tool to protect her from further injury in this relationship. Yet Annie was so entrenched in this image of the "good woman" that she could not access that emotion, even when it was justified and appropriate.

Annie had been taught by good Christian leaders that our lives are to be characterized by joy rather than defeat. Because of Christ's redemptive work, we have victory over depression, anxiety and anger. Her pastor sometimes preached against the "demon of depression." The underlying message Annie heard was that if she was a good Christian, praying

---

[2]Kathleen Fischer, *Women at the Well: Feminist Perspectives on Spiritual Direction* (New York: Paulist, 1988), p. 176.

and seeking God, then she would not feel angry, depressed or anxious. Annie was able to push down some of these emotions, such as anger, but she could not seem to get a handle on depression. She meditated on God's Word, prayed and sought Christian counsel, and yet her depression would not lift. Her inability to experience victory over depression increased her guilt, which in turn exacerbated her depression.

We do have victory in Christ over all things. At the same time, our world is a broken place filled with sin and pain. And it is in this broken world we live. Sometimes anger or sadness or worry is the only appropriate response to the world around us. We see this in the life of Jesus when he found men using the temple courts as a marketplace:

> So he made a whip out of cords, and drove all from the temple area, both sheep and cattle; he scattered the coins of the money changers and overturned their tables. To those who sold doves he said, "Get these out of here! Stop turning my Father's house into a market!" (John 2:15-16)

Jesus, when faced with the broken state of our world, did not become enraged or act out of control. But he also did not pretend to be happy about what he found in the temple. He did not put on a happy face. He did not avoid conflict. He did not pretend it was okay. He did not even diplomatically ask the sellers to stop their actions. Rather, Jesus, the perfect image of God, expressed his feelings directly to the men in the temple courts. He was perfectly genuine and authentic in his emotions.

In the same way, we honor God when we stop pretending and begin living authentically. God wants our whole selves—not ingenuine happy faces. We worship a loving Father, who looks at our pain with compassion: "Cast all your anxiety on him because he cares for you" (1 Peter 5:7). In this passage it is *assumed* that we will experience anxiety, and God gently invites us to lay our painful emotions at his feet.

When we walk through life with false proclamations of constant joy, we become less than real. I remember talking after my miscarriage to a friend who had suffered through years of infertility and four miscarriages of her own. "But it's all fine—I know God will provide," she constantly told me with a smile on her face. Although I respected and believed her trust and commitment, it felt plastic somehow. Surely she felt *something* about what she was going through. Of course God provides for his children, but it still hurts when our dreams are thwarted and our lives are falling apart; and it is okay to say that it hurts. "Often trust happens on the far side of despair," Brennan Manning writes.[3] Sometimes we feel pressure to get to the trust without ever feeling the despair. When we try to avoid painful feelings, we are also more likely to engage in destructive behaviors like substance abuse or promiscuity, which do not fix the pain, and cause problems of their own. What's more, it is often in the despair—or as St. John of the Cross referred to it, the dark night of the soul—that our trust becomes real and deep and honest.[4]

In order to have authentic relationships with God, characterized by genuine trust, we have to be honest with ourselves and with him. We cannot get to that place if we hide our angry, sad or anxious feelings. Instead, we need to trust that God views us with infinite compassion and loves us as we are—feelings and all. The Old Testament book of Psalms gives us numerous reminders that we need not withhold our painful feelings from God; rather, we can cry out and even groan in our distress:

> I cried out to God for help;
>   I cried out to God to hear me.
> When I was in distress, I sought the Lord;
>   at night I stretched out untiring hands
>   and I would not be comforted.
> I remembered you, O God, and I groaned;
>   I meditated, and my spirit grew faint. (Psalm 77:1-2)

We cannot be whole women if we do not acknowledge and accept our feelings, even the ones we wish we did not have. Perhaps the thought of

---

[3]Brennan Manning, *Ruthless Trust: The Ragamuffin's Path to God* (New York: HarperCollins, 2000), p. 77.
[4]See *Dark Night of the Soul,* trans. Mirabel Starr (New York: Riverhead Books, 2002).

embracing your anger, sadness or worry leads to some nagging doubts. *Embracing those feelings is just code language for whining and complaining about how bad I feel.* But when we genuinely embrace our feelings, it is not a complaint but a kind of confession—a humble admission of the truth of our current limitations. Only in acknowledging less-than-ideal feelings can we open ourselves up to learn from them and be moved to action and new growth.

One of the ways we can grow through painful emotions is to view them as signals or messages. Annie, who was unable to feel anger, might have benefited from anger's message. That anger might have told her that her needs were being ignored, that she was not being given the respect she deserved as a child made in God's image, and that she was worthy of being treated with love and care. It may have warned her against listening to false promises, reminded her of how many times those proclamations had been made in the past. Had Annie listened to anger's message, she might have been able to protect herself from further pain. I am not suggesting Annie was at fault in any way for her husband's infidelity, but had she been able to listen to anger, she could have potentially moved from a position of victim to an agent of change in her own life.

When we are overcome by painful emotions, it is worth listening to the messages they carry. The psalmist wrote, "In your anger do not sin; / when you are on your beds, / search your hearts and be silent" (Psalm 4:4 NIV). When we are faced with anger, anxiety or depression, we can silently search our hearts and ask ourselves what we can learn. What messages might God have for us here? I am not suggesting a simplistic cause-and-effect relationship, that if we listen to God's message and figure out the bad thing we did, then the pain will go away. However, as I will discuss more fully in chapter eleven, Scripture is filled with examples of how, regardless of *why* people are suffering, God teaches them through that pain. Instead of trying to wish away our anxiety or sadness, we should respect and pay attention to it.

Sometimes we are unable to hear the message in our pain because we have suppressed or quieted those emotional signals through alcohol, drugs, food or sexual indulgence. When we habitually turn to substances to numb our pain, we take away the possibility for growth. Instead of hearing what God could be saying to us through our sadness or worry or anger, we may try to bury it under a bottle of wine or a one-night stand. As Cornelius Plantinga writes, addiction keeps us from healing and wholeness:

> Addicts long for wholeness, for fulfillment, and for the final good that believers call God. Like all idolatries, addiction taps this vital spiritual force and draws off its energies to objects and processes that drain the addict instead of filling him. Accordingly, the addict longs not for God but for transcendence, not for joy but only for pleasure—and sometimes for mere escape from pain.[5]

Although addictive behaviors can provide temporary relief, they do not bring true healing. Unless we allow our pain to speak to us, we can never learn from it.

In my own experience, I was blessed to be surrounded by supportive people who encouraged me to be genuine and authentic with my painful feelings after my miscarriage. Being given the freedom to feel anxious and sad and angry, I was able to listen to those emotions and learn from them. My own grief taught me that, even though I love to talk about the importance of community and relationships, I often try to manage my pain by myself. However, even if I wanted to be self-sufficient after losing my pregnancy, I could not do it. A few days after my miscarriage, students were sharing prayer requests in one of my classes, and I began crying involuntarily. I have not cried in public since I was in elementary school—primarily because my face gets awful, red and puffy, and I get embarrassed. Yet I cried in my own class, and I received a gift. As relational beings, we grow and heal in the context of relationships, and that is exactly what happened to me. My students prayed over me that day;

---

[5]Cornelius Plantinga Jr., *Not the Way It's Supposed to Be: A Breviary of Sin* (Grand Rapids: Eerdmans, 1995), p. 131.

the young woman seated next to me quietly laid her hand on my back. That moment, in which I was able to accept the love and support of my students, was healing. Through my relationships with the students in that class, I received a touch of God's grace, compassion and tenderness. Had I pretended to be okay and ignored the message in my sadness, I would have missed God's gift of allowing others to carry my burden for me.

Learning to be honest about our emotions and view them as messages or signals can be a painful process, but pain is a wonderful teacher. Although it is not the teacher we probably request, most of us, in looking back on periods of intense growth in our lives, can see that those growth spurts were almost always preceded by seasons of pain. Parker Palmer discusses this growth through pain as he reflects on the impact of what he calls the "autumnal events" of his life:

> In retrospect, I can see in my own life what I could not see at the time—how the job I lost helped me find work I needed to do, how the "road closed" sign turned me toward terrain I needed to travel, how losses that felt irredeemable forced me to discern meanings I needed to know. On the surface, it seemed that life was lessening, but silently and lavishly the seeds of new life were always being sown.[6]

When we are faced with debilitating emotions and circumstances, that feeling of life "lessening" can be overwhelming. It is often only after we have journeyed through those painful seasons that we are able to look back and see the "seeds of new life" that were planted in those painful hours and feelings.

Painful feelings and circumstances change and shape us because "we know that suffering produces perseverance; perseverance, character; and character, hope" (Romans 5:3-4). This growth through refining fire is central to the Christian faith. In order to grow up into Christ, we must

---

[6]Parker Palmer, *Let Your Life Speak: Listening for the Voice of Vocation* (San Francisco: Jossey-Bass, 2000), pp. 98-99.

embrace seasons of pain as part of our journeys, as a way in which we share in Christ's sufferings. All of the people God uses are wounded and scarred, and the challenge of painful seasons—and of life in general if we are honest—is to find hope in the midst of despair.

COPING STRATEGIES

Although growth often comes on the other side of pain, this does not mean that we must stand idly by, looking for the message and waiting for the growth yet doing nothing to alleviate the suffering. We learn through the pain of physical illnesses, but we do not feel bad about taking antibiotics or following medical advice. When faced with debilitating anger, anxiety or sadness, we can learn through it, but we can also do something about it. We are not any less faithful when we use practical strategies to cope with difficult emotions or seek help from a counselor or doctor, particularly when those emotions are causing problems for us in our relationships, our workplaces or our schools.

The "Tools for the Journey" section is filled with practical interventions that I regularly use with clients who are struggling with these painful emotions. However, one of the most important steps we can take toward coping with anger, anxiety or depression is knowing when to seek counseling and support. Ask yourself the following questions to assess whether professional help is the healthiest next step for you:

- Do you experience depressed mood or excessive anxiety and worry most of the day, almost every day?
- Are you unable to experience pleasure during daily activities?
- Have you lost or gained weight unintentionally, or have you experience a marked change in your appetite?
- Do you have problems with sleep, such as difficulty falling or staying asleep, or do you want to sleep all the time?
- Do you experience fatigue or energy loss almost every day?
- Do you have panic attacks—periods of intense fear and discomfort, in which you experience symptoms like heart palpitations, sweating,

nausea, dizziness, chest pain, trembling, a fear of dying, etc.?

- Do you frequently experience irritability or muscle tension?
- Do you have problems with concentration, attention or decision making almost every day?
- Do you think about hurting yourself or taking your own life?

If you answered "yes" to three or more of the above questions—or if your anxiety, depression or anger are interfering with your relationships, job or school performance—then I would encourage you to seek counseling. Depending on the severity of your symptoms, you might be best served by a pastor, professional counselor or psychologist, physician, or some combination of the above. If your symptoms are in response to an identifiable life event and are not interfering significantly with your functioning, then your needs may be best met through a pastor or a lay counselor. When you need someone primarily to walk alongside you through your pain, someone to pray with you and support you, then a pastor or lay counselor may be exactly what you need.

Sometimes, however, you might need more than support: when your depression is so heavy that you can *feel* it like a weight on your back or in your chest; when you have no energy or interest in going to work, playing with your children, having sex, eating or even getting out of bed in the morning; when your fear and anxiety is so intense that you dread leaving the house; when you have masked your painful feelings with a substance, like drugs or alcohol, and are now unable to function without that substance; when you have panic attacks or flashbacks. If your anxiety or depression is interfering with your life in this way, you may feel hopeless. The good news is *depression and anxiety disorders are treatable*. One of the first things you can do to begin choosing life is to get the help of a professional therapist. Because depression and anxiety symptoms can be caused by underlying medical conditions, it is also important to consult with your physician. One of the things we know from research is that depression and anxiety are often related to an imbalance of certain biochemicals in the brain called neurotransmitters. Therefore, your physician or therapist may also recommend medication.

If you are unsure how to find a good, professional Christian counselor in your area, the following Christian counseling organizations have extensive referral lists and can connect you with a local therapist:

- The American Association for Christian Counselors <www.aacc.net>
- The Christian Association for Psychological Studies <www.caps.net>
- New Life Ministries <www.newlife.com>

TOOLS FOR THE JOURNEY

Practice living in the here and now. The first step toward freedom from depression and anxiety is learning to live in the present moment. This means that we are not trying to *escape* the moment (via alcohol, drugs, sex, food, etc.). Depression often involves a sense of living in the past. When we are sad, we are consumed with thoughts of broken relationships, personal failures and guilt over things done or left undone; all of these are events of the past. Anxiety, on the other hand, keeps us living in the future. When we are worried, we are overwhelmed by all the "what if" questions and fears; all of these are fears about what will happen in the future.

When you begin to get lost in your emotions, bring yourself back to the present moment. Practice this simple grounding exercise: take note of your senses. Ask yourself, *What am I feeling? seeing? hearing? tasting? touching? smelling?* Look for God in the present moment, and invite him to speak to you in the here and now.

Brother Lawrence, a monk who spent his days washing dishes in his monastery kitchen, wrote a wonderful book, *The Practice of the Presence of God.* [7] In this short book, he teaches us how to make every moment and every breath a living prayer to God. Read this book and meditate on its reflections as you make a conscious effort to begin living in the present moment.

---

[7] Brother Lawrence, *The Practice of the Presence of God* (New Kensington, Penn.: Whitaker House, 1982).

Learn to coach yourself toward healthy thinking patterns. When we feel anxious or angry or depressed, we tend to work ourselves up with our thinking, rather than coaching ourselves down. If we are worried about something, for example, our thoughts tend to spin the possible scenarios out of control. *What if I do badly on this test? What if I fail the class? What if I fail out of school and never get a job? I'll be a failure and will never be happy!* Consider how much worse each passing thought gets.

When you notice that you are beginning to get worked up in your thinking, silently remind yourself to *slow down.* Take several deep breaths, and visualize yourself as a coach. How can you, as a coach, help turn your thinking around? Review the thinking traps in chapter four, and identify those you fall into that tend to increase your difficult emotions. Name those thinking errors for what they are, and challenge your thinking.

Not only can you slow down and challenge your thoughts, you can also replace those thoughts with the truth of God's Word. Write reassuring Scripture on note cards and place them in visible spots, such as your bathroom mirror, refrigerator door or car dashboard. Even better, memorize passages to recite when you are getting discouraged. A passage that was really helpful to me after my loss was Lamentations 3:19-24, 31-32:

> I remember my affliction and my wandering,
> > the bitterness and the gall.
> I well remember them,
> > and my soul is downcast within me.
> Yet this I call to mind
> > and therefore I have hope:
> Because of the Lord's great love we are not consumed,
> > for his compassions never fail.
> They are new every morning;
> > great is your faithfulness.
> I say to myself, "The LORD is my portion;
> > therefore I will wait for him." . . .

For people are not cast off
　　by the Lord forever.
Though he brings grief, he will show compassion,
　　so great is his unfailing love.

I reminded myself that I would not be consumed and that his mercies are new every morning.

Search God's Word and find passages that speak to you, your situation, your feelings. Use God's Word as a shield around your heart. When we are told, "Do not be anxious about anything, but in every situation, by prayer and petition, with thanksgiving, present your requests to God. And the peace of God, which transcends all understanding, will guard your hearts and your minds in Christ Jesus" (Philippians 4:6-7), I do not hear a judgment against anxiety. Rather, I hear a loving God promising grace and peace for our broken and struggling hearts.

Make a growth timeline. One of the best ways to remind ourselves of how we have grown through seasons of pain is to do a conscious and intentional life review. Using a large piece of paper and starting with your childhood, note important events, memories, difficulties, changes. Be aware, however, that it is nearly impossible to return to the source of your wounds—even when you see the growth that happened on the other side of those wounds—without feeling some of that pain again. Many therapists like to tell clients that it may feel worse before it feels better. Yet it does get better—because even though reviewing old wounds can be painful, it can also remind you of who you are and how you got to this new, better place.

If you have been broken by tragedies like abuse, rejection, neglect or loss, and if you have never gone back to those wounds before, I would encourage you to do so with the help and support of a counselor. Although it is painful, it is worth returning to those broken places in order to celebrate the fact that you are a survivor! You are not a victim of your events or circumstances, but you are an amazing daughter of God who is growing and changing.

By making a personal growth timeline, you can get a vision of how God has used painful circumstances to shape and grow you. If you get discouraged or overwhelmed by your present pain, you can refer to your chart and remind yourself that "he who began a good work in you will carry it on to completion until the day of Christ Jesus" (Philippians 1:6). While this does not mean God *caused* those painful circumstances in order to teach you, this chart can be a helpful reminder that God makes beautiful things out of broken vessels.

Dip into the therapist's toolbox. In addition to these depth interventions, I also sometimes give my clients a number of practical tips on dealing with anxiety, depression or anger. What follows is a brief summary of each of those interventions:

Schedule your worry (or sadness, anger, etc.). Have you ever had someone quote you that song "Don't Worry, Be Happy"? Or have you ever had someone say, "You just need to relax," after you opened your heart and disclosed your anxious feelings? If so, you may have, like me, wanted to punch that person in the nose. But being a good Christian woman, you probably just smiled and nodded your head. The reason these comments are so frustrating is that, obviously, if you could just "be happy" or "relax," you would do it. But *how* do you do it? That is the million-dollar question.

Learning to relax can be a skill, and one way to practice that skill is to schedule your worry (or other painful emotion). The truth is that you are going to worry no matter what anyone tells you, so start scheduling it into your day. Give yourself fifteen minutes in which you do nothing but feel anxious, depressed or angry. When you find yourself getting anxious or depressed throughout the day, remind yourself of your appointment with worry later that day. This way you have a built-in container for emotions that are overwhelming. This is not a cure-all, but when you are overwhelmed by anxiety, this can be a great first step. When you see that your anxious feelings decrease even a little, you will get a taste of success, and nothing is more encouraging than your own progress.

Keep a feelings journal. One of the best things you can do to cope with painful emotions is to keep a journal. Write about your day. Write about what happened to you and how you feel. Often, when we write things down we can work them out in a way that we couldn't just by thinking or even talking about them. Writing requires us to focus our thoughts and helps us step outside ourselves to examine our feelings and problems objectively. With the help of a journal, you may just find new insights or new solutions to old feelings and problems.

Engage in pleasant activities. This is a simple strategy for a really difficult problem—people who are depressed do not engage in pleasant activities. So one way to help you get through some of those painful feelings is to identify some pleasant activities (such as having coffee with a friend, taking a warm bath, walking your dog, watching the sunset, etc.) and then set a goal of doing a certain number of pleasant activities every day.

Help someone else. Although this goes along with the belief that all altruistic behavior is essentially selfish in nature, nothing helps us get outside our own circumstances and feelings better than getting into someone else's pain. Find a way to help someone in need. Visit a retirement home, volunteer at a homeless shelter, do hospital visits with your pastor, tutor at-risk children. Do something for someone else. Both the activity and the needs of others may help you reframe your own experience.

Do relaxation exercises. If you struggle with anxiety or depression, you may have had someone tell you, "It's all in your head." Contrary to this incorrect and hurtful sentiment, anxiety and depression are problems we experience as whole selves—body, mind and spirit. We experience bodily symptoms of anxiety and depression, and sometimes one of the most helpful things we can do is bring our minds and bodies together for relief. A great way to do this is to use our minds to teach our bodies, through relaxation exercises, how to slow down and rest.

Many great books and websites are devoted to relaxation exercises, but you can get started by doing deep breathing. Lie down, close your eyes, and take several slow, deep breaths from your abdomen. To make sure you are breathing correctly, place one hand on your chest and the other below your ribcage. As you breathe, watch which hand rises and falls. When you are taking deep abdominal breaths the hand below your ribcage will rise and fall. Although this kind of deep breathing may seem like a challenge at first, it gets easier with practice and is the essential element of relaxation. In order to continue your relaxation exercise, breathe in abdominally for a slow count of three, then breathe out for a slow count of three. As you continue these deep breaths, walk yourself through each muscle group in your body. Practice tensing and then relaxing each muscle. Relaxation exercises aid in restful sleep and in stress reduction, and they can help with a number of mood symptoms as well.

Anger, depression and anxiety are painful. They are so painful that it is tempting to try and suppress or ignore them. Yet we cannot be and become whole women by growing through those emotions unless we acknowledge their presence, examine their messages and learn from them. I once co-led a group in which the other therapist gave each participant a rose when they entered the room. "The hardest part is often just showing up," she told them. You are already prepared to do some real work if you are reading this book; finding the strength to do the "Tools for the Journey" suggestions or being brave enough to seek help from a counselor reflects your inner strength. So be courageous, be encouraged and "just show up" as you allow God to grow you through experiencing your anger, anxiety or depression.

6

Never Good Enough

BUILDING HEALTHY SELF-ESTEEM

In our faithful listening to God's Word, we often neglect
his first word to us—the gift of ourselves to ourselves:
our existence, our temperament, our personal history, our uniqueness,
our flaws and foibles, our identity.
Our very existence is one of the never-to-be-repeated ways
God has chosen to express himself in space and time.
Because we are made in God's image and likeness,
you and I are yet another promise that he has made to the universe
that he will continue to love it and care for it.

BRENNAN MANNING
RUTHLESS TRUST: THE RAGAMUFFIN'S PATH TO GOD

I am blessed to have a very close relationship with my mom, although that may not have been obvious when I was a teenager. As a fifteen-year-old, I didn't understand how anyone could be as old-fashioned as my mother, and I probably shared these thoughts with her more than once. But even as an adolescent, I also talked to my mom about everything from boys to clothes to faith. In the years since I was an adolescent, our relationship has grown stronger. We still talk about clothes and faith, but now we also talk about balancing career and family, about being a good wife and mother, about gardening and writing. When I started working on this book, my mom was interested in every aspect of the process. As she learned about the topics I was going to cover, she was especially interested in this chapter. "That's me!" she exclaimed as I described the difficulty many women have in appreciating or even seeing who they are as infinitely loved children of God. Because she has given me permission to tell her story, I would like to tell you a bit about my mother.

My mother is smart and funny, compassionate and beautiful. She plays the piano and is a talented writer. She is a loving mother and has been the devoted wife of my father for forty-two years. Lacking a college degree but armed with a strong work ethic and matching competence, she went back to work after her four kids were in school and became a successful commercial loan administrator. My mother is also disciplined in her spiritual life, and the image of her reading her Bible at our kitchen table every morning challenges me to be consistent in my own relationship with God.

If you were to meet my mother and ask her about herself, however, you would not hear about these accomplishments or characteristics. She might tell you about her husband, her children or especially her grandchildren. If you said, "Yes, but tell me about *you*," she would probably struggle to give you an answer. If you went further and asked my mother about her strengths, she would have an even harder time. However, if you asked my mother about her weaknesses and limitations, she could give you quite a list. Like all of us, my mother is not perfect, but she is a woman made in the image of God with unique talents, skills and gifts.

Karen, a thirty-seven-year-old woman I saw in counseling for depression, also struggled with low self-esteem. Karen was a stay-at-home mom who spent her days doing essential but sometimes mundane household and childcare tasks. Although Karen had chosen to stay at home with her children, she felt insecure about her decision, especially around mothers who worked outside the home. Because Karen believed herself to be inferior and incompetent, she constantly worried that others were looking down on her, thinking she was old-fashioned or unable to keep an outside job. Even though Karen had been a high school valedictorian, this did not ease her insecurity. Karen even minimized that accomplishment, claiming that her school was not that difficult and her teachers had been easy. Karen constantly questioned her decisions, not only as a parent but as a wife, a friend, a neighbor and a church member. Like all of us, Karen longed for the love and acceptance of those around her. Yet she could not escape the feeling that she didn't really deserve that love and acceptance. No matter what she did, Karen felt like she could never be smart enough, funny enough, pretty enough, social enough, hospitable enough and so on. Although Karen was a committed Christian and an active church member, she was unable to see herself as a beloved creature made in God's image with unique gifts and talents.

Healing our relationship with self is an important part of the journey toward wholeness: "The purpose of salvation is to make whole that which is broken. The Christian spiritual journey settles for nothing less than such wholeness."[1] Sometimes what is "broken" is our concept of self. To be sure, we are sinful and fallen creatures, but we are also made in God's image and redeemed by Christ's love. God created us as unique beings with special talents and skills, but some of us, like my mom and Karen, have a hard time *believing* that God made us, knows us and loves us as we are. In the same way that people have problems in their relationships with God or others, some of us encounter difficulties in our relationship with self.

God created us in his own image, and we are "fearfully and wonderfully made" (Psalm 139:14). Looking inward to rediscover, accept and even celebrate the unique women God created us to be is not prideful or self-indulgent; it is not the same as bragging about accomplishments or

---

[1]David Benner, *Sacred Companions: The Gift of Spiritual Friendship and Direction* (Downers Grove, Ill.: InterVarsity Press, 2002), p. 36.

flaunting successes. Implicit in Jesus' teaching to "love your neighbor as yourself" is the need for love of neighbor *and* love of self (Matthew 22:39). As Brennan Manning writes, "We give glory to God simply by being ourselves."[2] We cannot glorify God by being ourselves when we do not even know that self! Unfortunately, many women lack knowledge and appreciation of the self God created.

In this chapter I will explore the concept of self-esteem, examining both what it is and what it is not. Many women do not experience the blessing of acceptance from parents, friends, spouses or—especially— from themselves. The world we as women grow up in provides important messages about how we should see, think and feel about ourselves. Therefore, I will explore the impact of relationships, culture and church on the development of self-esteem. I will also examine the life of Christ and, through his redemptive and empowering ministry to women, challenge you to reconsider how you think of yourself and how you can respond to the God who made you in his image.

LEARNING TO LOVE THE YOU GOD CREATED

During a recent visit to a friend's church, the pastor criticized the rise in popularity of Christian personal growth books because he suggested that they can lead people away from God toward an obsession with self. When you consider the task of building "healthy self-esteem," you may find yourself with similar concerns. Is "self-esteem" a euphemism for self-absorption and self-centeredness?

Self-esteem is not a bad word, nor is it equivalent to selfishness. Self-esteem simply refers to how we see, think or feel about ourselves. Some people have inflated self-esteem, in which they see themselves in an unrealistically positive light. Others have low self-esteem, in which they see themselves in an unrealistically negative light. When we examine the research on self-esteem, we find that women are more likely to possess the

---

[2]Brennan Manning, *Abba's Child: The Cry of the Heart for Intimate Belonging* (Colorado Springs: NavPress, 1994), p. 50.

latter.[3] Even though low self-esteem is a common problem for women, God did not create us to be harsh, mean and critical—to other people or to ourselves. "When I love myself," Susan Annette Muto writes, "it means that I love who I really am: a limited creature called to limitless joy; a fallible, finite being who can transcend sinful inclinations and seek the Infinite. It is this deepest self, this miracle of nature and grace, that I must esteem."[4] Part of growing in wholeness is learning to accept—and even love—the you God created.

A healthy level of self-esteem is neither unreasonably high nor low. Shelley, a close friend of mine, is a good example of a woman with healthy self-esteem. Shelley knows herself as a child of God and believes she has inherent worth. She does not think she is perfect and is aware of her weaknesses, but she is also cognizant of her unique strengths and talents. When someone criticizes her, Shelley does not respond defensively. Rather, she considers the feedback and measures it against what she knows of herself; she then tries to let go of those things that are not true of her while on the other hand learning from the difficult but accurate critiques. Shelley doesn't hide behind self-deprecating humor. She does not pepper conversations with self-critical remarks, thus inviting or even requiring the affirmation or encouragement of others. Shelley knows that not everyone agrees with the way she sees things, and she is okay with this. Although she enjoys being liked, she does not insist on the approval of everyone around her. This doesn't mean she is insensitive and uncaring. Rather, she is freed to do the work God has given her because she is not focusing her energy on protecting and defending herself or making sure that everyone likes and approves of her.

Like all of us, Shelley is not perfect. She makes mistakes and messes up; she hurts people's feelings and overreacts to things. But at the end

---

[3]Peggy Orenstein in association with the American Association of University Women, *Schoolgirls: Young Women, Self-Esteem, and the Confidence Gap* (New York: Anchor Books, 1994), p. xix.

[4]Susan Annette Muto, *Celebrating the Single Life: A Spirituality for Single Persons in Today's World* (New York: Image Books, 1985), p. 101.

of the day, Shelley knows who she is and is secure in her identity in Christ. How do we arrive at the place where we, like Shelley, respect and care for ourselves or, on the other hand, at a place where we question and doubt ourselves? We learn how to see, feel and think about ourselves from various sources growing up, and I will review three of those influences.

Our relationships. God created us in his image to be uniquely wired for interpersonal relationships, and it is in the context of those relationships that we do the most learning about ourselves. Developmental psychology research on early attachment indicates that the first relationship we experience, with our parent or primary caregiver, can have a profound impact on how we learn to see, think and feel about ourselves. Attachment theory is based on the observation that relationships are necessary for survival. Attachment research indicates that even when parents are neglectful and inconsistent, infants attach to their caregivers. Attachment figures are important because they provide a secure base from which their children can explore their environment, and they also offer a haven of safety to return to when faced with threat or danger. I saw this dynamic play out recently at the airport while a mother and her one-year-old son were waiting for their flight. The boy was walking along the corridor, but every few minutes he would stop and turn around to look for his mother. When he caught her eye, he would go back to his exploring, because he knew his secure base was still there. A few minutes later, the boy tripped and fell down, and he immediately turned and reached for his mother—a haven of safety to comfort him when distressed.

As children grow up they develop beliefs and expectations about the security and reliability of their caregivers based on repeated experiences. Attachment theorists refer to this set of beliefs and expectations as a child's *internal working model* of the attachment relationship, and it contains a model of both self and other. Therefore, if the boy in the airport has a consistently caring mother, he will develop an internal working model of a caring *parent* interacting with a lovable *self* who is able to get his needs met.[5] This internal working model becomes the earliest blueprint of self-esteem because it embodies our feelings and thoughts about ourselves and our ability to get our needs met in relationships. The internal working model is rooted in early experiences, but it is maintained or modified over time. Karen, my former client, was one of five children born to a critical and often absent father. Although Karen's parents loved her, Karen's mother struggled with depression and was not always available, either emotionally or physically. Karen thus developed an internal working model of an inconsistent parent interacting with a self who was unworthy of love. Over time, those beliefs were confirmed through repeated experiences with her parents. As an elementary school student running home to show off her report card filled with As and Bs, Karen remembers the embarrassment and disappointment she felt when her mother barely glanced at the card. *I could have done better,* she told herself. *Maybe my mother would love me if I was smarter.* Sometimes, though, Karen learned how to feel and think about herself through direct messages, such as her father's criticisms of her weight and appearance: "Karen doesn't need any dessert tonight—she's got enough meat on her bones as it is." Karen began to believe that if she could be thinner and more attractive, then maybe her father would be proud of her and love her. Not only was Karen's self-esteem affected by the words she heard growing up; it was also affected by what she did *not* hear. Although her parents loved her the best way they could with the resources they had, they were neither affirming nor demonstrative in their affection.

Of course, Karen's parents were not the only ones who influenced the way she learned to see, think and feel about herself. Karen's relationships with teachers and friends—and eventually romantic partners and even her own children—also influenced her self-esteem. But the early experi-

---

[5]For additional reading see John Bowlby, *Attachment and Loss,* vol. 1, *Attachment* (New York: Basic Books, 1969); also see Kimberly Gaines Eckert and Cynthia Neal Kimball, "God as a Secure Base and Haven of Safety: Attachment Theory as a Framework for Understanding Relationship to God," in *Spiritual Formation, Counseling, and Psychotherapy,* ed. Todd W. Hall and Mark R. McMinn (New York: Nova Science Press, 2003).

ences are so important because wounds that are rooted in childhood are often maintained in current relationships. Karen's internal working model—in which she saw herself as unworthy of love and unable to get her needs met—influenced her behavior and expectations with her parents and also with those around her. Her view of herself as unlovable became the *lens* through which she viewed all relationships. Karen believed she was unlovable and thought that she could never be pretty enough, smart enough or social enough for people to really love and accept her. More than anything, Karen, like all of us, longed for that love and acceptance. However, Karen did not believe she was worthy of love on her own, so she tried to earn people's love and affection. When she was agreeable and supportive, people seemed to like her, which actually ended up reinforcing her fear that people couldn't love her unless she was always pleasing to them.

Our relationships affect the way we see, feel and think about ourselves in numerous ways. The beliefs we develop about ourselves in the context of the parental relationship lay the foundation for our self-esteem, but those beliefs are maintained or strengthened over time with other relationships. Karen, believing from her earliest days that she was unlovable, tried to earn other people's affection. Unfortunately, she was so focused on being what other people wanted, she wasn't really sure who the real Karen was. Consequently, she tended to look to others, especially those closest to her, to tell her who she was. Somehow, in a genuine desire to love and be loved in return, Karen had lost the greatest gift she could give in relationships: herself.

When we look to others to tell us who we are, we are asking (maybe even demanding) for those closest to us to love and mirror us perfectly, to reflect our feelings and thoughts and abilities back to us with absolute accuracy and pointed insight. When they are unable or unwilling to do this, we can become depressed or angry. But when demanded from another human being, that desire for someone to tell us who we are sets us up for inevitable resentment. What we are really doing is asking that other person to be our god.

But only God can fully love or know us in this life (1 Corinthians 13:12). Other people cannot, will not and should not be that for us. Our husbands and friends and mothers can love us the best they can, affirm our strengths and remind us of who we are as children of God; they can help us see how God has designed us and how he knows us in Christ, but our true "mirror" is found only in God. As fallen human beings, we are destined to be hurt and disappointed in human relationships, just as we are destined to hurt and disappoint others. Only God can love us perfectly, and only by letting go of the expectation for others to fill that role can we rest in our true identity. When we love God and receive his love with no strings attached, then we can love others in return, without strings of our own.

Our culture. Although our relationships play a strong role in the development of self-esteem as we're growing up, our culture also provides important lessons about how girls and women should think or feel about themselves. Every time I teach a class on gender I play the song "When I Was a Boy" by contemporary folk singer Dar Williams. In her song, Williams weaves a story of a carefree girlhood filled with grass-stained clothing, topless bike riding and tree climbing. Without fail, several female students raise their hands after the song is over to describe with wide-eyed intensity how they, too, were tomboys. In the last verse, Williams describes a conversation with her boyfriend, in which *he* wistfully recalls his own boyhood days:

> When I was a girl, my mom and I, we always talked
> I picked flowers everywhere that I walked.
> And I could cry all the time, now even when I'm alone I seldom do
> And I have lost some kindness,
> But I was a girl too.[6]

This man describes some of the unique strengths attributed to femininity, including an ability to appreciate beauty, to communicate and to

---

[6]Dar Williams, "When I Was a Boy," *The Honesty Room*, Razor & Tie, 1995.

experience a wide range of emotions. Do you think my male students ever raise their hands to share their connection with these sentiments? Rarely! Even when they want to, our cultural vocabulary limits them. For example, while the girls can proudly proclaim they were "tomboys," what should the boys say? They were "sissies" or "girly"? Our culture teaches us that things masculine are better than things feminine. Therefore, girls can speak proudly about being tomboys, while boys who embody feminine traits are shunned.

As girls grow into women, we continue to see feminine things devalued. Although our nation has made great strides regarding gender equity, female college graduates still earn only seventy-three cents for every dollar that male college graduates earn. Even when we compare women in the same field, with the same degree and who are the same age, only half of women earn at least 87 percent of what the men earn.[7] Women also tend to be concentrated in lower paying jobs, so it is no surprise that almost twice as many women than men live below the poverty line.[8] Our culture measures value in money, and unfortunately, the dollars tell us that women are less important than men.

Equally damaging to girls and women, however, is the value our culture places on beauty and sexuality. In chapter seven, I will explore how this cultural emphasis on beauty can be damaging to body image, one important aspect of self-esteem. When Karen's father critiqued her appearance as a girl, she found confirmation that she didn't measure up in every magazine, television show and movie. Flooded with unrealistic images of perfect-looking women and surrounded by a culture that values women primarily for their appearance and sexuality, it should be no surprise that women are often plagued by a sense of inadequacy and low self-esteem.

Because we are fallen men and women, and in part because of our cul-

---

[7]Daniel E. Hecker, "Earnings of College Graduates: Women Compared with Men," *Monthly Labor Review*, March 1998, pp. 62-71.

[8]U.S. Department of Commerce, Bureau of the Census, *Income Poverty, and Valuation of Noncash Benefits, 1994* < www.unc.edu/~healdric/soci31/1998/assign/20facts.htm>.

tural heritage, we now find ourselves in a place where envy, jealousy and resentment can be found among both sexes. One woman is frustrated by what feels like an inability to climb the corporate ladder through the "good old boys" club and by the seemingly innocent but frequent comments her male colleagues make about her appearance. On the other hand, a man is frustrated after being passed over for a promotion he believed he deserved when a woman was hired to help with the gender inequity in the management team at his company. The negative consequence of this is that we begin to look at the relationship between males and females as a battle of the sexes. God designed males and females to be in harmonious relationship with one another. Self-esteem is found not through competition or devaluing one of the sexes but through working toward community and *shalom,* toward justice and peace between the sexes, where the voices and gifts of both males and females are heard and appreciated.

Our churches. We learn important lessons about how to see, think and feel about ourselves from our culture and our relationships. For many women, one of the cultural settings that teaches us these lessons is the church. Karen grew up with hurtful lessons from her parents, and she began attending church hoping to find safety and encouragement. Clearly this is what Jesus intended the church to offer: a sanctuary of hope, love and acceptance to broken, fallen, sinful people. Karen had already learned the importance of being what others wanted her to be, and so she paid close attention to the kind of woman who was praised in the church. That woman, Karen told me, was self-effacing, quiet, humble, a supportive wife and a diligent mother. She stayed at home with her children and supported her husband. She was agreeable, warm and friendly. Although Karen did not make a conscious decision to do so, she began slowly working toward becoming this "ideal" woman, rather than the unique woman God had created her to be.

When I asked Karen to tell me about herself at our first session, the lessons she had learned at church affected her response. Karen was afraid that focusing on or even acknowledging her talents was prideful and self-centered. Not only was pride a sin, but Karen believed that I would be unable to like or accept her if she acted this way. When churches unwittingly promote this kind of false humility, they are playing into a cultural double standard where confidence in women is labeled as vanity: "High self-esteem is an exclusively male prerogative. In men it is seen as a moral good, and a man who likes and values himself and lets the world know it is considered normal and is said to be demonstrating a healthy self-interest. But a woman who likes and values herself and lets the world know it is condemned for being vain, arrogant and conceited."[9] When we find it difficult to describe ourselves, who we are, what we like and even what we are good at, this does not reflect the Christian virtue of humility. Rather, it reveals a lack of good stewardship with the gift God has entrusted to us: the gift of ourselves.

We learn important lessons in the church not only by seeing the kind of woman who is affirmed and praised but also by the activities and roles that women have in the church. One of my mother's favorite stories to tell about my childhood reveals a lesson I learned when I was eleven years old. After moving to a new city, my mother asked me what I thought about the church we had been visiting. "I don't like it," I told her, "because the only thing they let the girls do is pass out the juice." My mother loves to tell this story with a punch line about how I became a feminist at a young age. But the truth of this situation is one that happens in many churches. The gifts of half of the church body are lost when women are not allowed to express their gifts unless they fit within accepted women's roles. When we look to our churches to tell us who we are and what we should be, we can be misled because churches are made up of broken and fallen people, just like you and me. To get an accurate sense of how Christ sees women and what he calls us to, we must examine the life of Christ and explore the message he offered women.

---

[9]Linda Tschirhart Sanford and Mary Ellen Donovan, *Women & Self-Esteem: Understanding and Improving the Way We Think and Feel About Ourselves* (New York: Penguin, 1985), pp. 3-4.

JESUS AND WOMEN

Because of Jewish law and custom, women in Jesus' day had neither rights nor respect in their community. Women could not inherit property, offer sacrifices, read the Torah, recite prayers or enter the temple's inner court.[10] Women could even be sold by their fathers, and if sold, they could not be freed after six years, as men could (Exodus 21:7; Leviticus 25:40). The Hebrew word for husband, *ba'al,* literally means "owner" or "master," and a man's wife was included in his list of possessions (Exodus 20:17).

Jesus, however, offered a radically different message about the importance of women through his words and actions. From his conception and introduction to the world to his resurrection, he repeatedly came to women *first.* In a patriarchal society that allowed a woman's father or husband to break her religious vow, God did not come to Mary's father or Joseph to tell them of Jesus' upcoming birth. Instead, God sent the angel directly to the young girl, Mary, and *she* accepted, "May it be to me according to your word" (Luke 1:38). When Jesus was ready to disclose his purpose and identity as the Messiah, he did not share this good news first with Peter or his other male disciples. Rather, while speaking to a woman whom other Jewish rabbis would have scorned—a Samaritan with a sexually sordid past and present—Jesus revealed himself as Messiah for the first time (John 4:25-26). After Jesus was crucified and buried, he rose from the dead and showed himself not to John, his beloved disciple, but to women. At a time when Jewish law did not even allow women to be witnesses in legal proceedings, Jesus commissioned those women to be his witnesses—the first evangelists (John 20:11-18; Matthew 28:8-10; Mark 16:9-11).[11]

---

[10]J. I. Packer, Merrill C. Tenney and William White Jr., eds., *Nelson's Illustrated Encyclopedia of Bible Facts* (Nashville: Thomas Nelson, 1995), pp. 421-31.

[11]For additional reading on Jesus' redemptive relationship with women see Mary Stewart Van Leeuwen, *After Eden: Facing the Challenge of Gender Reconciliation* (Grand Rapids: Eerdmans, 1993); see also Gilbert Bilezikian, *Beyond Sex Roles: What the Bible Says About a Woman's Place in Church and Family,* 2nd ed. (Grand Rapids: Baker, 1985).

Jesus did not treat women the way they expected a man and rabbi to treat them; instead, he offered them dignity, respect and tenderness, which surpassed their culturally conditioned expectations:

Jesus sees the unnoticeable women—the little gray shadows who make themselves invisible so that everywhere they can blend into the background, the inconspicuous silent sufferers who can only think of themselves as negligible entities destined to exist on the fringes of life. Jesus sees them, identifies their need and, in one gloriously wrenching moment, He thrusts them to center stage in the drama of redemption with the spotlights of eternity beaming up on them, and He immortalizes them in sacred history.[12]

Jesus saw women. I was reminded of the power and importance of this truth when a client came back from a conference she went to, where she spent the week in a small group with four other women. After each of the plenary sessions, they would break into their small groups. When she returned from the conference she told me, "It's amazing how you can get lost even in a crowd of four." When I examine Jesus' life, I find a God who does not allow us to get lost in the crowd, who sees us and values us even when we feel invisible and unimportant.

Rather than ignore women, degrade them or uphold certain patriarchal traditions of the Judaism of his day, Jesus preached to women and openly taught them in the court of women (Luke 21:1-4). He welcomed women as his travel companions and disciples (Luke 8:1-3). He presented women such as the poor widow as models of faith (Luke 21:1-4).[13] He almost never told a parable involving male images or activities without offering a parallel story his women followers could connect with through female images or activities. While Jewish law allowed men to be

---

[12]Bilezikian, *Beyond Sex Roles,* p. 82. Examples of these "unnoticeable women" include Peter's mother-in-law (Matthew 8:14-15); the hemorrhaging woman (Mark 5:25-34); Jairus's daughter (Mark 5:21-24, 35-43); the widow of Nain (Luke 7:11-17); and the crippled woman (Luke 13:10-17).

[13]Bilezikian, *Beyond Sex Roles,* pp. 85-87.

polygamous, Jesus instructed men to be monogamous and emphasized mutual responsibility in marriage.[14]

Jesus not only taught women, he also touched them during an age when some men were so against touching women they did not even allow women to count change into their hands.[15] Jesus healed women with his touch, like the woman crippled for eighteen years whom he called a "daughter of Abraham"—a term rarely used for women, although men were called "sons of Abraham" (Luke 13:16; 19:9). Even more striking is the fact that Jesus communicated such a deep love and respect for women that *women* felt comfortable touching *him*. Jesus even allowed a woman Luke calls a "sinner" to wet his feet with her tears, wipe them with her hair, kiss his feet and anoint them with ointment (Luke 7:36-50).

In the 633 verses in the Gospels where Jesus refers to women, he repeatedly challenges the negative cultural messages to women and offers instead a new message of hope and love. In the few passages that are negative, we are led to a deeper understanding of what Jesus values in women. For example, Jesus scolded Martha for busying herself in the kitchen with food, instead of sitting at his feet like Mary (Luke 10:38-42). Although custom kept women from learning the law, Jesus told Mary that she had chosen the better option. Another time Jesus was walking through a crowd and a woman cried out, "Blessed is the mother who gave you birth and nursed you." Jesus called into question her emphasis on a woman's role as mother over her more central identity as an image-bearer responsible to God. "Blessed rather," he told the woman, "are those who hear the word of God and obey it!" (Luke 11:27-28). Women responded to the message Jesus offered and were among his most loyal followers, standing among the Roman soldiers at the foot of the cross and appearing at Jesus' tomb early in the morning after the sabbath.

---

[14]Mary Stuart Van Leeuwen, *Gender & Grace: Love, Work & Parenting in a Changing World* (Downers Grove, Ill.: InterVarsity Press, 1990), p. 48.

[15]Letha Dawn Scanzoni and Nancy A. Hardesty, *All We're Meant To Be: Biblical Feminism for Today,* 3rd ed. (Grand Rapids: Eerdmans, 1992), p. 78.

We need to learn to see ourselves as Jesus sees us: individuals worthy of respect and love. When we find ourselves falling into the trap of believing that we can never be good enough, we are believing a lie. This truth is promised in Scripture: "There is now *no condemnation* for those who are in Christ Jesus" (Romans 8:1, italics mine). When we overemphasize our faults because we fear being prideful or because we have come to believe that those weaknesses define us, we condemn ourselves and do not honor God. When Jesus treated women as whole people, it motivated them toward change and action. Healthy self-esteem does not mean we will overestimate ourselves; instead, we will see our weaknesses and sins clearly when looking at ourselves through Christ's eyes. But we will also not focus on those sins and weaknesses to the exclusion of our God-given strengths and talents. When we know who we are—children made in God's image and redeemed by Christ's saving grace—we will be able to see ourselves honestly and with eyes of compassion.

TOOLS FOR THE JOURNEY

For those of us who have struggled with a lifetime of low self-esteem, the journey toward self-acceptance may seem impossible. We have spent years learning to see, think and feel about ourselves in the way we do now. Learning to be more gracious in our self-treatment will not happen overnight. Yet God calls us to see ourselves through his eyes, and these suggestions are a way to get started seeing ourselves "not just as we are by nature, but as we are by grace."[16]

Improve your self-knowledge. In order to build healthy self-esteem, you have to start with self-knowledge. Get to know yourself! Use your journal to respond to the following questions:

- Who are you? Open your journal and write down the first twenty words that come to mind when you hear this question.

- If I were to ask your spouse or best friend, how would he or she describe you? List the first ten words that come to mind.

---

[16]Anthony A. Hoekema, *Created in God's Image* (Grand Rapids: Eerdmans, 1986), p. 103.

- If you struggle with low self-esteem, you were probably tempted to fill up your journal with negative characteristics. Identifying your weaknesses is easy, so push yourself to go back through your journal entry and add two neutral or positive attributes for every negative characteristic you listed. *You are not just your weaknesses.* You are a whole person with gifts, talents and positive attributes.
- What do you like to do? What are your hobbies and interests? Describe at least five hobbies or interests.
- What are some of the special talents or gifts God has given you? What are you good at doing? Describe at least five strengths.

After reflecting on who you are, what you like doing and what you are good at, look for opportunities to live as the self God has made you. If you like bike riding, then make it a priority to go biking this week. If you enjoy writing, carve out time and prioritize that activity in your life. If you play the piano or enjoy hiking or softball, find time to engage in those activities. Set goals and celebrate your successes when you meet them. In addition, be a good steward of your talents and look for ways to use your strengths. If you enjoy teaching, look for places in your community or church to use that gift. Perhaps you do not enjoy being in front of people in a teaching role, but love listening to people and encouraging them. Use that gift to build relationships by becoming a youth leader or joining Big Sisters. If you are good with your hands and enjoy making things, help with art class at your child's school or volunteer with Habitat for Humanity. When we understand the unique gifts and skills God created us with, we are better able to enjoy those gifts by serving God and others.

Let go of The Perfect Woman myth. If you constantly compare yourself to an unrealistic ideal of the "perfect woman" in your mind, you are destined to feel like you will never be good enough. Likewise, if you constantly compare yourself to the standard of beauty set up for women in the media, you are destined to feel like you are never pretty enough. Even models are airbrushed into an unnatural perfection that they do not possess. In order to develop healthier and more balanced self-esteem, letting go of unrealistic expectations is a must.

We all have an ideal in our minds of The Perfect Woman. She is often a combination of the traits we saw affirmed in our families, our culture and our churches. Use your journal to write a description of the perfect woman in your own mind. Perhaps she sounds something like this: *The Perfect Woman? She's beautiful and well-dressed. If you stop by unannounced, The Perfect Woman is hospitable and warm, and her house is immaculate. Her kids always look perfect and, somehow, are never dirty, and they are always well-behaved. The Perfect Woman is also a warm and supportive wife. She is sexy without being provocative. She is incredibly smart and has an impressive career, yet she is a devoted and available mother. She is confident and spiritually insightful. The Perfect Woman is always friendly and kind, never irritable or impatient.*

After writing your description, ask yourself: who can live up to that kind of ideal? You might smile or even laugh a bit at the ridiculousness of your description. No one is like this! We are all human. We have weaknesses, inconsistencies and faults. But it is through those weaknesses and faults that Christ's power is made perfect, because in the midst of our own struggles, we learn and grow. Christ is able to redeem our mistakes and sins, as well as the sins that have been done to us, to make something good—in a creative way that only he can do (Genesis 37—50, especially 50:20). When you begin chastising yourself for not measuring up to that unrealistic ideal, extend grace to yourself. God calls us to sit at his feet and learn from him. Remind yourself of this when the self-doubts come, and lay the idol of The Perfect Woman at his feet.

Be nice to the kid in you. Do you remember what you were like as an eight-year-old? In order to begin healing the way you see, think or feel about yourself, you must look back to the source of those wounds. Examining the roots of hurtful childhood messages is not done in order to shift the focus and blame away from yourself and onto your parents or whoever hurt you. Rather, by looking back you can discover where you began to hurt yourself as you internalized those messages. A great movie to help you reconnect with your childhood is Disney's *The Kid*. Take some time to watch this movie, and then reflect on your own childhood: what you looked like, where you lived, who you lived with, what your parents were like, what school was like for you. How consistent or inconsistent were your parents? What were some of the hurtful messages you heard growing up? In what ways did you internalize those messages, and are you still carrying them around? How can you begin letting them go?

When we hold on to wounds inflicted by others and allow those people's distorted views of us to dominate our self-esteem, we do not allow God's truth of who we are to transform the way we think and feel about ourselves. Pastoral counselor John Patton suggests that forgiveness is a sign of positive self-esteem because "the victim is no longer building his or her identity around something that happened in the past. The injury is not all of who one is, but is rather a part of life that has at least started to move out of the center of the frame."[17] I will address forgiveness more fully in chapter ten, but it is important to note that unforgiveness can keep us stuck in the very things we wish to escape. In order to develop healthier self-esteem, we must begin to let go of some of those old wounds.

One way to begin letting go of hurtful self-evaluations is through visualization exercises. For example, if you, like Karen, grew up believing you were unlovable, look at a picture of a four- or five-year-old and imagine saying to that child, "You're unlovable!" Of course, you would never say that to a young child; instead, you would speak words of love. Now imagine yourself as the child in the picture, and speak the kind words to yourself that you needed to hear (but didn't) from a parent or friend growing up.

Regardless of the *source* of your unhealthy self-esteem, the way you see, think or feel about yourself is maintained by *you*. In order to develop healthier self-esteem, you have to change the way you think about your-

---

[17]John Patton, "Forgiveness in Pastoral Care and Counseling," in *Forgiveness: Theory, Research, and Practice*, ed. Michael McCullough, Kenneth Pargament and Carl Thoresen (New York: Guilford Press, 2000), p. 290.

self. You can know that you have internalized negative messages—whether they came from your parents, your siblings, your church or culture—when you have begun believing and acting as if those negative messages are true. As I discussed in chapter four, we repeat those messages to ourselves as negative self-talk.

So remind yourself to be gentle in the way you talk to yourself. If a good friend was berating herself for not being beautiful or smart enough, what would you say to her? Would you agree and tell her that she's right, that she doesn't deserve to be loved? No! You would challenge those thoughts, responding with love and encouragement. When that negative self-talk gets going, reframe those thoughts. Try a little tenderness in your self-talk! Gently remind yourself to stop focusing on the hurtful messages from the past. Reorient yourself to the present situation and look for ways to use your strengths and skills to cope with life in the present moment. Focus on what you can do and how much you have already done, instead of on your limitations and weaknesses.

Given what you have read about Jesus and his treatment of women, what might he say to you in those moments when you are attacking yourself? Spend some time meditating on the simple fact of God's amazing love for you. Let yourself sit and invite God to fill you with his love and presence. Listen to the words of Henri Nouwen: "All I want to say to you is, 'You are the Beloved,' and all I hope is that you can hear these words as spoken to you with all the tenderness and force that love can hold. My only desire is to make these words reverberate in every corner of your being—'you are the Beloved.' "[18] Devote time to meditating on these powerful words: *you are beloved.*

After meditating on God's unfailing love, which runs higher and deeper and broader than we can imagine (Ephesians 3:18), imagine what God would say to you. Write a letter to yourself that reflects God's love for you. You might want to use Scripture, hymns or song lyrics in your

---

[18]Henri Nouwen, *Life of the Beloved: Spiritual Living in a Secular World* (New York: Crossroad, 1992), p. 26.

letter. Post it on your mirror or your refrigerator, and when you become discouraged and defeated, feeling like you will never be good enough, read that letter. Replace those unfair, irrational, negative self-cognitions with the truth of your identity in Christ and God's love for you.

Our relationships, our culture and our churches offer many messages about our value and importance. When those messages are unreasonably negative, and when we internalize them and believe that we are defined by our weaknesses and faults, we do not honor who we are and who we are becoming as people made in God's image and redeemed by Christ's love. In order to grow in wholeness, we need to know who we are as women of God and be secure in that identity. With a balanced view of self, we will be free to serve God and others by living out the gifts and callings God has placed in us.

7

Doing Battle with Your Body

DEVELOPING A HEALTHY BODY IMAGE
IN A TOXIC BODY CULTURE

They weren't wearing cover-ups either, but they were lovely
and firm as models—I'd say that was the main difference—
and all in bikinis. Two of them were already perfectly tan.
And suddenly my trance was broken.
Suddenly it was the Emperor's New Clothes, and I stood there
in all of my fatitude like the tubby little emperor
with his feta-cheese gut. In my mind now I looked like someone
under fluorescent lights and felt in comparison to these girls
like Roy Cohn in his last days. I wanted a trapdoor to open at my feet.

ANNE LAMOTT
TRAVELING MERCIES: SOME THOUGHTS ON FAITH

Do you weigh yourself daily, or do you avoid the scale at all costs
and dread doctor visits because of the painful and embarrassing
weigh-in? Perhaps you opened to this chapter hoping to discover
some new and effective weight loss tip. Or maybe you are tempted to

skip this chapter because of the deep shame and guilt you have about yourself and your body. Perhaps regardless of the actual health of your body you cannot escape the feeling that you and your body are never good enough.

This is a feeling I know well. When I was twenty years old, I discovered that I was considered medically obese, meaning 20 percent or more over the healthy weight for my height. This was devastating to me. Although I had never been particularly skinny as a young teen, I began putting on weight with alarming speed in late high school. As a college freshman, I gained the "freshman 15" and then some. Discovering that I was no longer just "overweight" but actually "obese" was a wake-up call for me.

I had tried a seemingly endless number of weight-loss programs and felt utterly defeated. But somehow, during my junior year of college, I was able to lose weight the old fashioned way: by eating less and exercising more. I don't have a simple formula for how I did this, but I know I didn't do it on my own. Only through the strength of Christ was I able to walk through that life-changing experience.

When I was in the process of losing weight, I was flooded with women confessing their personal struggles with emotional eating, food addiction, eating disorders, low self-esteem and negative body image. I could not believe how many women—beautiful, healthy women—were plagued by their own critical internal voice. However, I also could not believe how differently people treated the overweight me—people like pastors and church members, professors and supervisors, bank tellers and grocers, friends and family members—from the non-overweight me. While I couldn't help but enjoy the positive attention I received, I was deeply grieved that it took a physical change to feel respected for the internal woman I always was.

If you have ever felt unhappy with your body and gained weight or lost weight—or tried to gain or lose weight—you are obviously not alone. "I pretty much avoid looking in mirrors," Kate, a thirty-three-year-old female, told me early on in our counseling relationship. "I constantly compare myself to other women, and I never measure up. I hate having sex with my husband because I'm embarrassed by my body, and I'm sure he's disgusted. I tell myself I'll be good today. I'll exercise and eat healthy, but I get discouraged and depressed. I mess up, and it starts all over again."

As a therapist I have shared in the heartbreak of women like Kate who are in a constant battle with themselves and their bodies. As a Christian woman who has struggled with what it means to have a healthy weight and body image, I have often wondered about the proper Christian understanding of the body. If the body is the temple of the Holy Spirit, then how are we to think about and treat the body? Is counting calories or carbs or fat grams a sign of vanity? Body image issues are particularly important for American women, given the social epidemic of eating disorders, the high obesity rates in the United States, the negative impact that dieting has on the body, and the unrealistic expectations our media and culture set up for us regarding weight and appearance.

In chapter six, I explored self-esteem in general; in this chapter I will examine one particular aspect of self-esteem: how we think and feel about our bodies. Examining the cultural messages that Western women receive beginning in girlhood about our bodies and what they *should* be, I will present Christian perspectives on the body. God created us as whole people—with unity of body and spirit. We grow in wholeness when we celebrate the reality that God has created us as embodied creatures. Therefore, to battle against our bodies (for not being thin enough, attractive enough, curvy enough, etc.) is to battle against our*selves*— God's good creation.

A Beautiful Body: The Yellow Brick Road to Acceptance?

It is no wonder that American women feel unhappy about their bodies. The average fashion model today is 5'11" and weighs 117 pounds, whereas the average American woman is 5'4" and weighs 140 pounds.[1]

---

[1]"Media Bombards Women with Mixed Weight Messages," *Consumer Health Journal* (October 2003), citing statistics from the Alliance for Eating Disorders Awareness, retrieved at <www.consumerhealthjournal.com/articles/women-and-weight.html>.

This discrepancy leads many girls and women to feel ashamed and critical of their bodies. As a result, we do anything we can to attain the unattainable. We learn this at a very young age. Mary Stewart Van Leeuwen, in her book *After Eden,* provides the results of multiple studies to illustrate the guilt that girls and women feel about their bodies. According to one study, 50 percent of nine-year-olds and almost 80 percent of ten- to eleven-year-olds were on diets because they thought they were too fat.[2] By the time girls turn into women, their dissatisfaction is even stronger, as 75 percent of American women think they are overweight!

Why do we react so strongly to the cultural message that we need to be unnaturally thin? Perhaps one reason is because in terms of social acceptance we are correct in believing that big is bad. Van Leeuwen argues that men are not perceived as fat unless they are more than thirty-five pounds overweight, whereas women are considered fat if they are between ten and fifteen pounds overweight. "Few obese women are treated with the respect that many fat men still receive," says Van Leeuwen, "especially if they [men] are wealthy and/or powerful."[3]

Additionally, Mary Pipher points to research on social desirability to illustrate the bias against obesity in American culture. According to one study, 11 percent of Americans said they would abort a fetus if told it had a tendency toward obesity. Another study found that elementary school children have more negative attitudes toward obese children than toward bullies, handicapped children or children of different ethnicities. Teachers have been found to underestimate the intelligence of fat children and to overestimate the intelligence of thin kids.[4]

From a very early age, Western girls are faced with the implicit message in the media that they must be ultrathin to be accepted. This message is reinforced for many by parents, siblings and other extended fam-

---

[2]Mary Stewart Van Leeuwen, *After Eden: Facing the Challenge of Gender Reconciliation* (Grand Rapids: Eerdmans, 1993), p. 269.

[3]Ibid., p. 270.

[4]Mary Pipher, *Reviving Ophelia: Saving the Selves of Adolescent Girls* (New York: Ballantine Books, 1994), p. 184.

ily members. In school, girls observe how their obese classmates are treated by their teachers and peers, and this message is further confirmed. "Girls are terrified of being fat," Pipher writes, "as well they should be. Being fat means being left out, scorned and vilified. Girls hear the remarks made about heavy girls in the halls of their schools. No one feels thin enough."[5]

When faced with these strong messages about what we should look like and the reality of what happens to those of us who fail at this, girls and women do whatever it takes to be thin. According to Pipher, when "unnatural thinness became attractive, girls did unnatural things to be thin."[6] What is unnatural? I believe it is unnatural that *ten million* women in the United States alone have an eating disorder such as anorexia or bulimia. While an eating disorder is the most extreme consequence of this unattainable cultural ideal, millions more women suffer from the negative effects of constant dieting. Some argue that the negative health consequences of excess weight justify the means of dieting. However, other research indicates that constant dieting places *more* stress on the body than being twenty pounds overweight.

Like all women, Christian women are also taught from a young age that the body is important because it is the standard by which we are judged. If we are thin and attractive, then we will be liked. The damaging consequence of this imbalanced valuing of appearance is that many girls and women learn to do whatever it takes to be thin and attractive in order to experience that love and acceptance. Is there, however, another way to look at the body? As Christians, we are called to be in the world but not of the world. What would an "other world" perspective on the body teach us?

WHOLE PEOPLE: SOUL AND BODY

Throughout history, some have argued that the importance of the body

---

[5]Ibid.
[6]Ibid.

lies in its (subordinate) role as a vessel for the (more important) soul, but this does not accurately reflect God's creation. As discussed in chapter two, God created us in his image as whole people, people with a *unity* of body and spirit. As theologian Colin Gunton writes, "The image of God embraces our embodiedness as much as our intellect and 'spirituality.' "[7] In other words, our bodies are just as important to our status as image-bearers of God as our minds or souls. We are ensouled bodies as much as we are embodied souls.

Our bodies are important, therefore, because God *created* us in his image as embodied persons. It is not by chance that we are physical beings. Some theologians point out that our physical bodies provide a constant reminder of our fundamental need for relationship as beings made in God's image: "Individual existence as an embodied creature entails a fundamental incompleteness or, stated positively, an innate yearning for completion. This sensed incompleteness is symbolized by biological sex—that is, by existence as a particular person who is male or female."[8] Our bodies, which are anatomically made for physical connection with another human being, remind us of our need for relationship and our longing for wholeness.

Not only did God choose to create us as embodied humans, he also chose to *reveal* himself to us in the form of an embodied human person, Jesus Christ. Christianity is an incarnational—a bodily—religion. "God made human beings to be embodied creatures," Cornelius Plantinga writes, "and the second person of God honored us by assuming our flesh and blood."[9] Therefore, we know the body is important because God became an embodied creature to reach us. God also chose to *redeem* us through the physical death and shedding of Jesus' blood: "But now he

---

[7]Colin Gunton, *The Promise of Trinitarian Theology* (Edinburgh: T & T Clark, 1991), p. 118. See also Vaughan Roberts, *God's Big Picture: Tracing the Storyline of the Bible* (Downers Grove, Ill.: InterVarsity Press, 2002), pp. 27-28.

[8]Stanley Grenz, *The Social God and the Relational Self: A Trinitarian Theology of the Imago Dei* (Louisville, Ky.: Westminster John Knox Press, 2001), p. 277.

[9]Cornelius Plantinga Jr., *Engaging God's World: A Christian Vision of Faith, Learning, and Living,* (Grand Rapids: Eerdmans, 2002), p. 37.

has reconciled you by Christ's physical body through death to present you holy in his sight, without blemish and free from accusation" (Colossians 1:22). And finally, we know the body is important because God is going to *resurrect* the body (1 Corinthians 15:35-44). We are not intended, therefore, to disdain or hate or wage war against our bodies. Rather, we are to present our bodies as "living sacrifice[s], holy and pleasing to God" (Romans 12:1).

When we devalue our bodies or act as if they are only important because they house our souls, we do not take seriously who and what God has made us to be: embodied relational persons in his own image. However, when we become preoccupied with our bodies, when our thoughts and feelings are more directed toward how we look than toward who God is and what he is saying to us, then we allow our bodies to become gods. And our bodies can become gods whether we are young or old, attractive or unattractive, overweight or underweight. As Brennan Manning writes:

> Honesty requires the truthfulness to admit the attachment and addictions that control our attention, dominate our consciousness, and function as false gods. I can be addicted to vodka or to being nice, to marijuana or being loved, to cocaine or being right, to gambling or relationships, to golf or gossiping. Perhaps my addiction is food, performance, money, popularity, power, revenge, reading, television, tobacco, weight, or winning. When we give anything more priority than we give to God, we commit idolatry. Thus we all commit idolatry countless times every day.[10]

Idolatry can come in many forms. Food can be an idol, but looking good, either physically or spiritually, can also be an idol. Our bodies are important, and we honor God not by being fixated on our appearances, but through valuing and honoring our bodies as part of God's good creation.

One way we can honor God's good creation is by seeing ourselves as

---

[10]Brennan Manning, *The Ragamuffin Gospel: Good News for the Bedraggled, Beat Up, and Burnt Out* (Sisters, Ore.: Multnomah, 1990), pp. 83-84.

a whole, instead of focusing on a part of ourselves—such as our physical imperfections or even on those things that make us look different from others. My friend Becky has taught me about the value of seeing myself as a whole. Becky is a beautiful woman who happens to have a reddish birthmark covering much of her right arm and hand, as well as a small part of her upper back. As a little girl, Becky noticed that her skin looked different from the other kids, and so when she took a bath she would try to scrub off her birthmark. Her mother would explain to her that her birthmark was part of her and that it wouldn't go away with scrubbing. Now that Becky is an adult, she likes her birthmark and no longer tries to scrub it away. Her husband loves it, and she sees it as a part of who she is. Becky looks at herself as a whole person—and her birthmark is one part of that whole self.

Potential traps await us: obsession with our bodies or body hatred, extreme dieting or food addiction, excessive exercise or emotional eating. Jesus demonstrated a balanced whole life, in which physical and spiritual needs are both respected and met. Neither was valued over the other. Jesus came "eating and drinking" (Matthew 11:19), but he also fasted and taught his followers to do the same. In the Sermon on the Mount, Jesus said, "When you fast . . ." (Matthew 6:16)—not *if* you fast but *when*.

In Romans 14:6, Paul wrote, "Those who eat meat do so to the Lord, for they give thanks to God; and those who abstain do so to the Lord and give thanks to God." This is my prayer for your spiritual and physical life, as well as my own. When I eat, I want to be able to give thanks to God because I am not choosing a god *before* him. Rather, I am honoring him in the way I eat. And when I fast, I want to be able to thank God that he has enabled me to sacrifice my desire for food in order to honor him.

TOOLS FOR THE JOURNEY

If you misuse your body by treating it poorly and/or hating it, then you cannot honor and reflect God fully, so let's discuss several ways to grow in your capacity to mirror God as an embodied human person.

Focus on what you can do (instead of what you look like). You can do amazing things. Your skeleton replaces itself every three months. Your liver replaces itself every six weeks; your skin every month; and your stomach lining every five days. If you doubt your remarkable nature as an embodied person, consider conception and pregnancy. A woman can nurture and sustain the life of an unborn child from the time it is just a tiny mass of cells until it is a seven-pound baby. Anne Lamott, in her book chronicling her son's first year of life, writes, "I'm going to have an awards banquet for my body when all of this is over."[11]

Instead of focusing on what you *look* like (or don't look like), begin to focus on what you can *do.* Sometimes, however, the very reason you might be frustrated with your physical body is because of what it *cannot* do. Perhaps because of disability or illness, your mobility is limited. I have learned about the impact of this in a new way since my mother-in-law had a stroke four years ago. She has very little feeling on the left side of her body, but through perseverance and an incredibly strong will, she has learned to walk with a cane and do any number of things one-handed that I would have thought impossible, like floss her teeth and chop vegetables. Although my mother-in-law looks forward to a new body in heaven—one that is cancer-free (oh yes, she had breast cancer too) and stroke-free—she somehow finds a way to still live in gratitude. When my mother-in-law watches her grandchildren playing on the floor, I am sure that her longing to get down and play with them feels like an ache in her heart, but she also finds a way to enjoy all the gifts of her existence as an embodied creature— the sloppy kiss of her grandson, the sweet smell of the Gerber daisies that her husband planted for her, the sound of her son's voice over the phone, the tender touch of her husband as he helps her to bed. My mother-in-law is not able to do many of the things she would like to do, but her gratitude for what she *can* do motivates her to keep moving forward and allows her to enjoy the gifts and blessings in her life.

---

[11]Anne Lamott, *Operating Instructions: A Journal of My Son's First Year* (New York: Anchor Books, 2005), p. 59.

Make a list of specific things you can do. Your list might include things like:

- I can breathe (don't underestimate the amazing creative power infused in the simple act of your bodily existence!).
- I can eat, sleep and drink.
- I can feel pain, letting me know when something is wrong or dangerous.
- I can play tennis or take the dog for a walk.
- I can smell strong coffee, fresh daisies, my mother's skin.
- I can conduct a conference call, participate in a meeting, teach a class.
- I can hug a friend or play with a child.
- I can feel a warm summer breeze on my face.
- I can write letters and send e-mails.
- I can nurse my baby, change her diaper, rock her to sleep.
- I can laugh and cry and talk.
- I can repair a computer system or play the piano or mow the grass.
- I can make love to my husband.

Affirm yourself for these things—you really are remarkable! As you begin to appreciate yourself for what you can do, not just for what you look like, you'll be motivated to try new things. For example, after I started running, I was able to appreciate my legs for being strong enough to support me even when I'm tired, rather than focusing on the imperfections of their shape or size.

When you begin reciting body-hating messages, remind yourself that you were created as an embodied person in God's image and look for ways to turn the negatives into positives. For example, if you dislike your wide hips, try reframing that thought into a positive appreciation, such as, "Thank you, God, for making me a woman with curves—curves designed by you to nurture and sustain life. Thank you, God, that my curves remind me of how very much a woman I am." Even if you're feeling skeptical, you might be surprised how a little gratitude can change your perspective. When I look down at my post-pregnancy stomach and feel the negative body messages cueing up, I try to close my eyes and remember what that belly looked like with my precious baby boy living inside it. Things aren't exactly the same there now, but I like to think of my new stomach as a reminder of the gift of motherhood. This doesn't mean I buy out the Ben & Jerry's ice cream at my local grocery store and stop exercising in celebration of my baby-making body. Rather, I find that I want to be nicer to myself when I think of my body in this way.

Practice focusing on what you can do, instead of what you look like, and my guess is you will begin making healthier choices as you learn to love and appreciate yourself as an embodied person made in God's image.

Honor God with your behavior. God has created us with bodies that tell us important things, like when we need food or drink. If you abuse your body by your behavior, you cannot fully reflect God's image in you. For example, if you chronically overeat, this behavior does not honor God. Behaviors like chronic overeating are about trying to fill up an emptiness inside you, but they just don't work. In the Sermon on the Mount, Jesus says, "Blessed are those who hunger . . . for they will be filled" (Matthew 5:6). Chronic overeating, especially in its most extreme form—binge eating—is the opposite; it is typically accompanied by neither physiological hunger nor satisfaction. I used to constantly overeat and never feel satisfied, and one of the greatest gifts of the physical changes I experienced was rediscovering what real hunger and satisfaction felt like. While this was my particular struggle, abuse of the body comes in many forms: self-starvation, binging and purging, excessive exercise, chronic dieting.

When we maltreat ourselves by undereating or overeating, we do not honor God. Begin monitoring your physical hunger. God has made you with a body that gives you clear signals to let you know when you are hungry and full, thirsty and satisfied. Take a day when you can eat according to your body's signals (versus convenience, impulse or pre-arranged dieting mealtimes). Wait to eat until you feel the physiological signs of hunger. Do you know what those hunger pains feel like? Perhaps you know those pains well from chronic dieting, or you might have ignored them for so long that you don't even notice them anymore. Remind yourself of the beauty of your body's signals. It's amazing how much your body will tell you if you listen to it. When you do feel hungry, eat! Try to eat slowly so that you can continue to listen to your body. Be aware of each bite of food and drink plenty of fluids. When you begin to feel full, stop eating. When you begin getting frustrated with your appearance and are tempted to slip back into unhealthy patterns, remind yourself that your body is not the enemy. Rather, God created you purposefully as an embodied human being. Perhaps go back to the previous step, and begin listing again what you can do, instead of just thinking of your body in terms of appearance. Ask God to allow his truths to penetrate your core and overrule those self-critical thoughts.

Learn about God through bodily activities. You can learn about God through pleasurable activities (such as walking through nature or seeing a sunset), and you can also learn about God through activities that challenge you physically. By pushing yourself to power walk or jog for two miles, to lift weights for fifteen repetitions or to ride the exercise bike for thirty minutes, you can learn about "press[ing] on toward the goal to win the prize" in a new way (Philippians 3:14). When you push yourself through *temporary* physical pain to attain a goal, God can teach you powerful object lessons about perseverance and endurance.

You can also learn about God through self-denial. The list of characters in the Bible who model self-denial and fasting is lengthy, but John the Baptist is one prime example, "for John came neither eating nor drinking" (Matthew 11:18). Churches don't talk about fasting as a spiritual discipline too often anymore. We'd rather talk about the more "spiritual" disciplines like prayer and meditation. But isn't it really just because fasting is too hard? What would we do at those church potlucks if everyone was fasting? Lisa McMinn makes the observation that "it would seem that wherever two or three are gathered in God's name, there in the midst of them is food."[12]

Through fasting you learn something about God that you simply cannot learn through *thinking about* fasting. Richard Foster, in his classic book on the spiritual disciplines, *Celebration of Discipline,* writes this about fasting: "More than any other Discipline, fasting reveals the things that control us. This is a wonderful benefit to the true disciple who longs to be transformed into the image of Jesus Christ. We cover up what is inside us with food and other good things, but in fasting these things surface."[13]

Feeling hunger and choosing to deny that need is powerful. If you fast, you may be painfully reminded of your earthly and human nature. There is also a mystery in fasting. Through what looks to the outside world like a very physical and tangible exercise, you can experience an intense inner transformation and revelation of God's Spirit.

Let me offer a few words of warning regarding fasting. First, if you are someone who has a history of excessive food restriction as a means of dieting (i.e., starving yourself), then fasting is not the best vehicle through which to meet God. I would suggest that you could perhaps meet God more powerfully through eating and finding peace in doing that which you have considered off-limits in the past. Second, please don't fast while harboring secret thoughts of dieting. Fasting is not dieting. If your real motive in fasting is to lose a few pounds before the weekend, you're going to miss the joy and the lesson in fasting. If you choose to fast, do so for the experience and process of fasting—to seek and listen to God—not for physical bodily changes.

Look at your body as a whole. God has created us as whole people, and God has created our bodies as whole bodies. We will grow in our search for wholeness when we stop breaking our bodies into pieces that

---

[12]Lisa Graham McMinn, *Growing Strong Daughters: Encouraging Girls to Become All They Meant to Be* (Grand Rapids: Baker, 2000), p. 128.
[13]Richard Foster, *Celebration of Discipline: The Path to Spiritual Growth* (San Francisco: Harper San Francisco, 1988), p. 55.

we like and don't like. For example, "I have nice eyes, but my arms are chubby," or "Pretty smile, but too-skinny legs." You have a whole body. Start trying to think of and appreciate your body that way—not as a bunch of imperfect parts thrown together.

Let's review some practical suggestions on ways you can begin to appreciate your body as a whole:

- Buy clothes that fit the *real* you right now, not the fantasy you that is ten pounds less or six workouts away. Don't wait to lose those ten pounds to buy a nice swimsuit or a pretty dress for your vacation. Wear clothes that are comfortable and that you feel good in.

- Make a list of ten things you like about yourself that have nothing to do with your appearance. You are an embodied person, not *just* a body. Post this list on a mirror to remind you of your value when you start attacking yourself.

- Take time to figure out what makes your whole self feel good, and then *do* those things. Perhaps you'll soak in a bubble bath or enjoy a warm cup of tea in a soft robe and slippers by the fire. Maybe you'll splurge and get yourself a full-body massage, a facial or a pedicure. Pursue knowledge about yourself. What feels good? And then follow up by treating your whole body well.

- If you constantly compare yourself to other women, begin by not comparing yourself to airbrushed models and adolescent girls in low-rise jeans. Instead, look at the real women around you—all of them, not just those that are skinnier or more fit than you. Begin admiring real women in stores and restaurants, focusing on what they can do, not just what they look like. Treat them with the same kindness you are learning to treat yourself with.

- Stop filtering out the positive information you get about yourself. Don't just focus on and internalize the negative messages you pick up about yourself from others. Allow yourself to accept positive feedback, and incorporate those things into your view of yourself as well.

- Pay attention to how much of your negative self-talk is about your body. Put your thought-stopping into practice, and replace those thoughts with items from your list of things you appreciate about yourself. For example, if you are constantly telling yourself, "I've gained too much weight. Nobody will like me when I look like this," remind yourself of all the reasons people *will* and *do* like you, such as, "People like me because I'm a kind person. I am thoughtful. I am a loyal friend."

As you journey toward wholeness, remind yourself that your body is not the enemy. When I am getting ready for a date with my husband and checking myself out in the full-length mirror in my closet, I often struggle with this war-mentality as I mentally attack various aspects of my body. But let me encourage you to join me in your effort to stop waging war with your body! Instead, remind yourself that your body is part of how you are "fearfully and wonderfully made" (Psalm 139:14).

Reflect for a moment on how much time you spend thinking about your appearance: what you look like, what you wish you looked like or, perhaps, what you used to look like. What would happen if you channeled that time and energy into something more productive? We are not meant to worship our bodies, ignore them, misuse them or hate them, but to embrace them. Make a commitment to not waste any more time hating your appearance and treating yourself badly. God intentionally created us as embodied people, and we grow in wholeness when we begin appreciating God's good creation.

PART THREE

Growing Outward

8

Rethinking Female Sexuality

SEXUAL INTIMACY, SINGLE SEXUALITY AND SEXUAL WOUNDS

*Sexuality is good—a wonderful gift that drives us
toward intimacy with another and reflects the intimate communion
we long to have with God. However, like all good things,
the fall led to distortions of our sexuality.*

LISA GRAHAM MCMINN
*GROWING STRONG DAUGHTERS:
ENCOURAGING GIRLS TO BECOME ALL THEY'RE MEANT TO BE*

ex sells. Sex is used to sell everything from movie tickets to magazines, from jeans to cigarettes, from cars to cola products. Hollywood paints a seductive picture of sexuality, but that picture is distorted and damaging. Our culture is obsessed with sex. Consider just a few of the popular television shows of the past decade: *Sex and the City,* a drama/comedy centered around the sexual escapades and adventures of four girlfriends in New York City; *Friends,* a comedy about friendships and romantic relationships built around sexual jokes and innuendos; or *Alias,* a spy show featuring a gorgeous woman pulling off amazing feats in stiletto heals and a push-up bra.

We cannot watch the news or flip through a magazine without being assaulted by advertisements that sexually objectify women. We cannot check our e-mail or surf the Internet without provocative advertisements popping up on our screens. Women are objectified in advertising, but that objectification goes even deeper in pornography, which has reached the masses in a new way with the Internet. No longer do people have to buy magazines hidden behind the counter or risk being seen visiting an adult bookstore. Instead, with the click of a button, fulfillment of almost any sexual fantasy is immediately available.

If we blindly listen to our culture and accept the messages popular movies, magazines, television shows and advertising promote about sex in general, and female sexuality in particular, then we may begin to believe that sexual pleasure in any context is more important than trust, commitment and integrity. If we are seduced by these popular images, we may begin to feel inadequate about everything from our sex drive to our appearance in the bedroom to our sexual performance. Unfortunately, many of us do unwittingly buy into these cultural myths and then feel embarrassed by our inadequacies and fearful that our husbands are unsatisfied. When the reality of our bedroom experiences does not measure up to the unrealistic fantasies created by Hollywood, we feel disappointed and ashamed.

When we consider the sexual obsession in our culture, it should perhaps be no surprise that sexual sin is damaging people, that sexual abuse is ravaging lives, and that sexual addiction is ruining marriages—both inside and outside the church. With all the ways in which sexuality has been distorted, it is tempting to view sexuality with suspicion. Sex can be (mis)used to damage people and relationships. It can rip marriages apart and steal away purity and innocence. It tempts our husbands, our parents, our friends and ourselves. It can lure us into unsafe territory that maligns our loyalties and distorts our expectations. Yet the truth is, sex was created by God, and it is good.

God created us as sexual beings, and our sexuality is expressed in two dimensions. First, God created us as gendered beings with male or female bodies. Second, God created us with the potential for sexual relations—a potential designed to be expressed within the boundaries of marriage. The sexual act has both a spiritual aspect (when it is good and right to be sexually active) and, obviously, a bodily aspect, involving a man and a woman using their respectively male and female bodies. The first dimension—our identity as gendered beings—is a gift given to all, and it is to be enjoyed and used to serve others whether married or single. On the other hand, the potential for sexual relations is a part of being human, but sexual activity itself is not necessary for human wholeness. Jesus came to us as a whole male human being with masculinity, male physiology and the potential for sexual relations. But being fully human did not require him to marry or become sexually active in any way. Both these dimensions of our sexuality are somewhat distorted by the Fall and can be further misused by our own choices. Therefore, we need Christ's healing in both these dimensions, whether single or married.

God could have created all human beings the same, but he chose to sexually differentiate males and females. Growing up, our Sunday school teachers probably did not focus on this aspect of our personhood, but the reality is that God *chose* to create us as sexual beings in his own image. As Lewis Smedes writes, "Traditional talk about the image of God in man hardly gives a nod to human sexuality; it assumes that we are God's image in spite of our bodies, not *as* bodies. To zero in on sexuality as the God-like in us seemed to insult God."[1] Our sexual differentiation reminds us that we are made for relationships and are fundamentally incomplete on our own. Like two pieces of a puzzle, the male and female anatomy fit together. This does not mean that singles are incomplete without a partner. Rather, our sexuality reminds all of us, whether married or single, that we are incomplete without God. As Susan Annette Muto writes, "Understood spiritually, to be single is a sign of the basic incompleteness of this life. To live this vocation is to remind others that

---

[1]Lewis Smedes, *Sex for Christians: The Limits and Liberties of Sexual Living* (Grand Rapids: Eerdmans, 1976), p. 31.

no human love can fulfill us totally. There is more that the human heart sees, and this More is God."[2] God intentionally created us in such a way that our physical bodies provide a constant reminder that we are ultimately and always oriented toward connection with another.

In addition, God could have made people reproduce in any number of ways, but God chose to create sexual intercourse: an act that can bring intense intimacy and ecstatic pleasure. Smedes goes on to point out that sexual intercourse reflects how God has made us in his image: "Sexual intercourse—at its best—is an epitome of the responsive life of persons in communion."[3] The sexual act "at its best" is experienced within the context of marriage. When a husband and wife give of themselves sexually to one another, they reflect who they are as "persons in communion." Sexuality (our sexually differentiated bodies and our natural desire for sexual intimacy) and sex (intercourse) are created by God. As such, they are not dirty or shameful, but good.

Human sexuality, both our biological sex and our potential for sexual relations, is a gift that teaches us something important about who God is and how he has made us, but it has also been twisted and distorted by the Fall. In this chapter I will examine three ways that our sexuality, in both dimensions, has been distorted. Under the conditions after the Fall, the experience of our sexuality can be shameful, violating and even used sinfully. Thankfully, Jesus came to earth to reverse the effects of the Fall and heal that which is broken. Therefore, we will also explore how we are forgiven and how God restores, purifies and makes whole our sexuality—whether we are married or single, sexually active or celibate.

MARRIAGE AND SEXUALITY IN A SHAME-FILLED WORLD

Ann, a thirty-five-year-old woman—who initially came to counseling for anxiety—eventually disclosed that her "real" reason for seeking help was

---

[2]Susan Annette Muto, *Celebrating the Single Life: A Spirituality for Single Persons in Today's World* (New York: Image Books, 1985), p. 179.
[3]Smedes, *Sex for Christians*, p. 33.

a long-term struggle with sexual intimacy. Even though Ann knew she was supposed to enjoy sex with her husband, she had never experienced any real sexual pleasure. Ann dreaded lovemaking, but she had been having sex with her husband once or twice a week for their ten years of marriage. Ann viewed sex as a duty she was obligated to perform to be a good wife, as well as marital insurance so her husband would not seek pleasure elsewhere. Ann loved her husband and wanted to have an intimate relationship. She knew her low sex drive and inability to experience orgasm or pleasure was keeping her from being able to enjoy an important aspect of intimacy. She also knew her lack of pleasure was a source of disappointment and insecurity for her husband.

Abstinence was highly valued in Ann's family and church, and she was taught from a young age the importance of saving herself sexually for marriage. Ann adhered to this teaching and was a virgin on her wedding day. Unfortunately, the underlying messages Ann had picked up about sexuality did not magically disappear after the wedding ceremony. "I grew up thinking of sex as dirty. Listening to married women joke about their husbands fixing things around the house in order to 'get lucky,' I thought sex was for the man," Ann told me. "It seemed like women had sex to please their husbands, rather than to experience pleasure themselves."

After having sex for the first time, Ann was distraught by her physical pain as well as her emotional shame. She knew intellectually that sex in marriage was supposed to be beautiful, but she could not rid herself of her embarrassment and guilt. After Ann came back from her honeymoon, she had lunch with an unmarried friend who was living with her boyfriend. The friend talked explicitly about her boyfriend's pleasure with her ability to experience multiple orgasms. Ann felt even more ashamed and a bit betrayed. Ann had waited for marriage to have sex, but her sex life was not even painless, much less pleasurable. She insisted on turning the lights off during intimate moments because she was embarrassed for her husband to see her naked body, and her inexperience made her feel clumsy and insecure. However, she was too ashamed to talk to her husband or anyone else about her frustration and guilt.

In addition to these messages about the sex act itself, Ann was also taught important lessons about her sexual body. Women's menstrual cycles and reproductive issues were always spoken about in hushed tones in Ann's home. When Ann got a yeast infection as a teenager, her mother referred to Ann having a problem "down there." Ann learned that her sexual organs were inherently dirty and that she should not even talk about them by name. These feelings of shame about her sexual body were in addition to her feelings of inadequacy about her body in general. Ann longed to be able to be naked and unashamed with her husband, but she never felt thin enough or attractive enough—regardless of her husband's affirmation of his love for her and attraction to her.

When our sexuality is surrounded with feelings of shame, this can negatively affect our desire for sexual intimacy, as well as our pleasure during lovemaking. Ann is not alone in her struggle with sexual desire; approximately 33 percent of women suffer from a very low desire for sex, known as hypoactive sexual desire disorder. Some women even find sex repulsive or disgusting. Twenty-four percent of women suffer from female orgasmic disorder, in which they have extreme difficulty reaching orgasm. Pain during intercourse is not uncommon when women first become sexually active, but some women experience excessive pain during intercourse for years. This can have physical roots, but it can also be caused or exacerbated by anxiety and fear during sexual activity. Approximately 20 percent of women experience occasional pain during intercourse, but 14 percent of women suffer from dyspareunia, or chronic genital pain associated with sexual activity.[4]

God created us as sexual beings, and the ability to experience sexual desire and pleasure is a gift from him. Yet many women are unable to receive that gift. Because of the Fall and its further sinful aftershocks, the experience of our sexuality is often accompanied by shame, but this

---

[4]J. R. Heiman, "Sexual Dysfunction: Overview of Prevalence, Etiological Factors, and Treatments," *Journal of Sex Research* 39, no.1 (2000): 73-78; E. O. Laumann, A. Paik and R. C. Rosen, "Sexual Dysfunction in the United States: Prevalence and Predictors," *Journal of the American Medical Association* 281, no. 13 (1999): 1174.

need not be so. A redemptive view of creation understands that sexuality, in and of itself, is good. The sexual act, in and of itself, is good. Our bodies, including our sexual organs, are good. We do not need to, nor should we, reject, suppress or ignore our sexuality. Rather, we should love and embrace our sexuality as an essential aspect of who we are, whether we are seventeen or seventy-five. Sex is not a duty we must perform for our husbands. It is not something we are obligated to do so our husbands will stay close to home. God created us in such a way that we too can experience the heights of physical pleasure in the form of sexual orgasm. "That God gave us bodies that *could* experience such incredible physical pleasure ought to encourage us to embrace sex as wholly good within the context of a deeply committed relationship," writes Lisa Mc-Minn. "A discomfort with sex reflects the brokenness of our sexuality. To seek help if we find ourselves disgusted and unable to enjoy the pleasure of sex is to seek wholeness."[5]

Sexual dysfunction for both men and women may be strongly related to a medical problem. Consulting a physician is a practical and essential step in addressing sexual difficulties. Women, of course, are not the only ones who suffer from sexual dysfunctions. Contrary to the messages emanating from popular movies and television, men are not always interested in sex, nor are they always ready and able to perform sexually. When our husbands experience sexual difficulties, this is painful for both partners. In this book I am focusing on the negative cultural messages and attitudes toward women, but equally damaging pressures exist for men. In the movies and on television, leading men are sexually virile and physically powerful, ready for sex at a moment's notice. Behind closed doors, however, many of us have discovered that this stereotype is far from a reality for the leading men in our own lives. In fact, half of all men experience difficulties achieving or maintaining an erection at least some of the time. Approximately 10 percent of men experience

---

[5]Lisa Graham McMinn, *Growing Strong Daughters: Encouraging Girls to Become All They're Meant to Be* (Grand Rapids: Baker, 2000), p. 168.

chronic difficulties with erectile dysfunction, and that number increases to at least 15 percent for men over age sixty. In addition to erectile dysfunction, approximately 30 percent of men experience premature ejaculation, and 8 percent of men suffer from orgasmic disorder.[6]

Male sexual dysfunctions, like female ones, can have physical roots, but they can also be exacerbated or maintained by stressors such as infertility or aging, marital problems or a history of abuse, low self-esteem or fear of hurting one's partner. When men struggle to perform sexually, whether through an erectile dysfunction, premature ejaculation, painful intercourse or low sex drive, this can affect their self-esteem as well as our own. We may be overwhelmed by self-blaming thoughts: *Why isn't my husband sexually attracted to me? There must be something wrong with me that he doesn't want to be intimate with me. I always knew I was ugly, and this only confirms it—even my husband is disgusted by my body and can't be aroused by me.* These thoughts are a natural response to the pain of a disappointing sexual relationship, but they also keep us from joining with our husbands to find healing.

When we are faced with the pain of a sexual relationship that is less passionate or fulfilling than we hoped it would be, we need to partner with our spouses on the journey toward sexual wholeness. Just as we have wounded and tender parts in our souls, our husbands also have wounded and tender spots in their souls. Because of the cultural pressures for male sexual bravado, a man who is struggling sexually may feel particularly ashamed. As wives, we can add to our husband's shame or we can offer him the healing balm of tenderness and compassion. Real intimacy is found between people who feel safe with one another. When we are gentle and loving with our husband's most vulnerable and secret struggles, we offer him the deepest kind of love and safety. Treating our husbands with gentleness is allowing Christ to do his redemptive work—replacing shame with confidence in the goodness of sexuality.

---

[6]Heiman, "Sexual Dysfunction," pp. 73-78; Laumann et al., "Sexual Dysfunction in the United States," p. 1174.

If you or your spouse are encountering difficulties in your sexual functioning, whether because of disinterest or even disgust with sexual activity, because of erectile dysfunction or premature ejaculation, because of inability to experience pleasure, or because of chronic pain during intercourse, then you should know that these sexual dysfunctions are very treatable. Seek support from a qualified therapist who specializes in sex therapy, or pursue help through a Christian sex therapy book or video. The Sexual Wholeness Institute is a comprehensive Christian center for sex therapy, and it offers a variety of resources—including books, videos and workshops—through its website <www.sexualwhole ness.com>. Sex was not intended to be painful or unpleasant. It is a good gift from God! Growing in wholeness means embracing all aspects of yourself, including your sexuality. If you are struggling in your sexual relationship, ask your husband to join you in a journey toward sexual wholeness.

WHEN SEXUALITY IS USED TO VIOLATE WOMEN

Although sex and sexuality are good, one result of the Fall is feeling shame about our bodies and ourselves as sexual beings. Like our original parents, we want to hide our nakedness (Genesis 3:7-10). However, an even more damaging result of the Fall is when something that God has created for good is used to wound. The most profound and disabling example of this is sexual abuse. When people are sexually abused, the core of their personhood is damaged. Being introduced to sex and sexuality this way is a vivid example of how sin corrupts and distorts that which is good and beautiful. God created us as sexual beings, and our sexuality reminds us of our inherent need for relationship with others and, ultimately, with God. Sexuality is an essential aspect of how we have been made in God's image, and it is precisely because our sexuality is so important that sexual wounds damage us so deeply. Unfortunately, sexual abuse is all too common. Finding reliable statistics on the prevalence of sexual abuse is difficult because it is often underreported. Researchers also differ on how they define sexual abuse (e.g., the required age difference between offender and victim, maximum age for victim, etc.). With all the difficulties of measurement in mind, most professionals estimate that between one in three and one in four girls are sexually abused in some way by the age of eighteen.[7]

Sexual abuse is not the only way sexuality is misused in our fallen world. As girls and women, if we are pushed to do *anything* sexually we are uncomfortable with—from a friend, a boyfriend or even a husband—this silences our voice and diminishes our sense of self. In addition to the damage caused when our significant others push us to do things sexually, it is also violating when our boyfriends or husbands focus their sexual energy on other women. If our partners are fighting a losing battle with lust—whether through illicit relationships, fantasies about other women or pornography—this demeans and devalues our sense of personal worth and integrity.

Sex and sexuality are gifts, and they are good. But when sex is used to violate our basic rights—our right to be safe, our right to choose when we will experience sex for the first time, our right to fidelity, our right to choose how and what we will do sexually—then sex becomes a weapon. When women have been sexually violated, whether through sexual abuse, unwanted sexual experiences or a partner's sexual indiscretions, they feel shamed and dirty. I am not suggesting that a husband looking at Internet pornography a few times is the same as years of childhood sexual abuse, but I do believe that any kind of sexual violation leads to feelings of guilt and shame. Jesus brings healing to our deepest wounds, and when those wounds mean our sexual purity and integrity has been ripped away, our hope is for purity.

If you have been sexually abused, it is easy to disconnect from yourself—from your innocence, your vulnerability and your sexuality. But you cannot find healing and wholeness without rediscovering those hidden parts of yourself. That means going back—back to a painful place

---

[7]U.S. Department of Health and Human Services, "Child Sexual Abuse: Intervention and Treatment Issues," Child Welfare Information Gateway (1993) <www.childwelfare.gov/pubs/usermanuals/sexabuse/sexabuseb.cfm>.

that you would probably rather forget. Yet as long as you avoid those dark places in your life, they retain power over you. In *The Courage to Heal*—a classic book for women survivors of childhood sexual abuse— the authors suggest that the path to healing is not easy or painless, but it is straightforward: "All you need is the safety and support that enable you to go back to the source of your pain, to feel the feelings you had to repress, to be heard, to be comforted, and to learn to comfort yourself."[8] Making this decision to "go back to the source of your pain" may seem overwhelming. But the choice *not* to go back is a choice not to heal, not to grow, not to live.

Sexual abuse can lead to disconnection not only from self but also from God and others. When we are lost in pain, we often spend our energy trying to protect ourselves from future pain. However, when our lives are focused on avoiding things and people that could potentially hurt us again, we also miss out on the joy of living. Jesus offers so much more. In John 10:10 he tells us, "The thief comes only to steal and kill and destroy; I have come that they may have life, and have it to the full." If you have experienced the trauma of sexual abuse, you have had much stolen and killed and destroyed in you. Despite the work of the destroyer, Christ has already worked to restore and redeem you, so let me encourage you to take Christ's hand to begin the healing process. Only through engaging in that process of intentionally working through your pain will you ever be able to have life "to the full." If someone has violated you sexually, it can seem near impossible to trust others. For example, if you were raped or abused or coerced by a male, it might be tempting to view all men as potentially dangerous and untrustworthy. This kind of black-and-white thinking is self-protective—some men (and some women) *are* dangerous—but it is also inaccurate: not all men (or all women) are dangerous. The life Jesus promises is a life lived in community. In order to answer that call to live in community, it may be help-

---

[8]Ellen Bass and Laura Davis, *The Courage to Heal: A Guide for Women Survivors of Child Sexual Abuse* (New York: HarperPerennial, 1988), p. 120.

ful for you to employ the support and guidance of a trained and experienced Christian therapist to partner with you on your healing journey.[9]

In contrast to those women who experienced sexual abuse or unwanted sexual experiences in their past, others are living with the trauma of sexually addicted husbands who are trapped in a secret sexual world right now. If your significant other has had physical or emotional affairs, or has struggled with addiction to pornography or masturbation, these secret behaviors are violating to you. The path toward healing is a complicated one, because you are not the only one involved in the hurtful relationship. Seek the support of a professional therapist, preferably one who specializes in sexual addictions. Some churches offer support groups for spouses of individuals with sexual addictions, which would also be helpful as you begin your healing journey. If your husband has a sexual addiction, developing an understanding of his struggle can also be helpful.[10] If you are not married but are choosing to stay with a boyfriend who is violating you by his actions, professional counseling is especially important for you to be able to explore boundaries, any hidden motives to "save" your partner, or the possibility of damaging patterns repeating themselves in your current relationship.

For your own healing, you must allow yourself to grieve—the loss of hope, loss of trust and, perhaps, the loss of your relationship. Healing may involve making decisions about your future and how best to protect yourself and your children. When your husband violates you sexually,

---

[9]I highly recommend reading a book on recovery from childhood sexual abuse, along with pursuing personal counseling. Dan Allender's book *The Wounded Heart* (Colorado Springs: NavPress, 1990) offers a uniquely Christian approach to healing. You can also purchase a workbook that includes guided journaling exercises and other activities. Two other classic sexual abuse recovery books are Wendy Maltz, *The Sexual Healing Journey: A Guide for Survivors of Sexual Abuse* (New York: Harper, 2001); and Bass and Davis, *The Courage to Heal,* which also has a separate workbook with structured activities (New York: Harper & Row, 1990).

[10]Several books provide a thorough examination of sexual addiction, such as Stephen Arterburn, *Every Man's Battle: Winning the War on Sexual Temptation One Victory at a Time* (Colorado Springs: WaterBrook, 2000); and Harry W. Schaumburg, *False Intimacy: Understanding the Struggle of Sexual Addiction* (Colorado Springs: NavPress, 1997). Books specifically written for wives of sex addicts include Laurie Hall, *An Affair of the Mind* (Wheaton, Ill.: Tyndale, 1996); and Marsha Means, *Living with Your Husband's Secret Wars* (Grand Rapids: Revell, 1999).

through his actions toward you or toward others, this is not the way God intended you to experience sex. It is meant to be a beautiful and safe expression of intimate love. When that safety is violated, it is deeply painful. Although Jesus offers healing, this does not mean your husband will necessarily be changed. The only change you can guarantee is the one you pursue for yourself, and that growth process comes through having the courage to take Jesus' hand and courageously walk through your pain and betrayal with him. How individual people find healing is, to some degree, a mystery. There is no easy formula, and our explanations only go so far. But we know that through Christ, healing *is* possible.

SEXUAL SIN PREVENTS SEXUAL WHOLENESS

Sexuality has been distorted by shame and violation, but it has been warped in another important way, and that is our own sinfulness. We cannot have an honest discussion about sexuality in a fallen world without exploring the role of personal sexual sin. Culturally we have learned to squirm at the mention of the word *sin,* but it is a reality of our world. In fact, it is *the* reality of our world. Part of the reason we struggle to feel whole sexually is because of sin—and not just sin in general, but also our own sin. Our screw-ups. Our mistakes. Our regrets. We do things we should not do, and we think things we should not think. As much as we may want to live lives of integrity and purity, if we are honest with ourselves, we do not always do it. We fall down and mess up, over and over again.

Even though we know we are imperfect, it is uncomfortable to look at our own sin. Our culture has offered us many distractions away from an honest inward examination of personal sin. Yet to talk about sex without talking about sin is more than likely going to be a superficial conversation. Psychologist Mark McMinn suggests we have exchanged the deep language of sin for a shallow language of popular psychology:

> It is good to explore parent-child relationships, look for biological explanations, and understand dysfunctional family relationships.

But none of these things should dismiss the language of sin. While some repeat the mantra, "I'm OK, you're OK," it is much wiser to conclude, "I'm a mess, you're a mess." We're all caught in the midst of a sinful world that manifests itself in our biology and our close relationships as much as our willful choices.[11]

McMinn does not suggest we do away with psychotherapy, but he does argue that a journey toward growth that ignores our own sin is an empty one. If we want to understand how our sexuality has been distorted by the Fall, we must examine our own sexual sin.

We are called to sexual purity: "Flee from sexual immorality. All other sins people commit are outside their bodies, but those who sin sexually sin against their own bodies. . . . Therefore, honor God with your bodies" (1 Corinthians 6:18, 20). We are called to honor God with our bodies and live lives of sexual purity, but we fall short. "Sin offends God not only because it bereaves or assaults God directly," Cornelius Plantinga writes, "but also because it bereaves or assaults what God has made."[12] The specific ways we can sin sexually are endless, but whether we were sexually promiscuous teenagers or went farther than we wish we had with our fiancés, we "bereave and assault" both God and what God has made (like us and our partners) when we sin sexually, and the wounds stay with us. I think of my friend Kathleen who fell in love at age eighteen and got pregnant after having sex for the first time with her boyfriend. They had only dated a short time, but Kathleen and her boyfriend got married and now have three children. Yet Kathleen still struggles with chronic guilt over her past sexual sin and is constantly trying to make up for those sins by good deeds, whether through volunteering at church, babysitting for neighbors or helping out at her children's schools. Yet no matter what she does, she never feels like it is enough to compensate for her sin.

---

[11]Mark McMinn, *Why Sin Matters* (Wheaton, Ill.: Tyndale, 2004), p. 20. McMinn is referring to Thomas Harris's 1974 book, *I'm OK—You're OK.*

[12]Cornelius Plantinga Jr., *Not the Way It's Supposed to Be: A Breviary of Sin* (Grand Rapids: Eerdmans, 1995), p. 16.

Kathleen is right. Like all of us, she can never do enough to fix herself. Our hope lies not in our good deeds, which can never bridge the gap to the perfection God demands. When we try to find solace in our goodness, we are bound to be disappointed. We hope not in our ability to save ourselves, but in the one who saves us. The good news of Christianity is that Jesus came to Earth to reverse the effects of the Fall and redeem that which is ugly and broken and distorted. Jesus heals our wounds and forgives our sins, and he gives back that which was stolen. Jesus' perfect life and his subsequent death served to satisfy God's justice that sin not go unpunished. Through his Son taking on our punishment, we are free from the eternal consequences of our sin and God is able to work to redeem our pain and sin. However, when we have sinned sexually, we can get caught in a web of lies: *I don't deserve to get married because I did not obey God and remain sexually pure. I don't deserve to have a sexually fulfilling relationship in marriage because I did not wait until marriage for sex. If I had honored God with my body before marriage, then I would be able to enjoy sex now. Sexual unhappiness now is God's way of punishing me for my disobedience.*

If God forgives us, he *forgives* us. God promises that when we confess our sins, he is faithful to forgive us and purify us from *all* unrighteousness (1 John 1:9). God does not punish us with sexual pain or displeasure. In order to embrace God's forgiveness, we have to believe him. Believe his promise. Believe that he fully sees our sins and completely forgives them. Only by accepting God's forgiveness can we forgive ourselves and move forward to live in freedom and joy. Of course, God's forgiveness does not remove natural consequences of sin. When Kathleen knelt beside her bed as a frightened teenager and confessed her sin, she also pleaded with God to keep her from getting pregnant. Although she did not receive the answer she hoped for—that God would disallow the consequence of her sin—God built something beautiful in Kathleen's family out of what began in shame and regret.

Sometimes, however, we do not confess our sin. We are so afraid of God and ashamed of our sin that we try to hide it from God. Yet the amazing truth about God is that he is never surprised by our sin. We cannot shock him. We cannot do anything so awful that he will reject us or leave us. As J. I. Packer writes, "There is tremendous relief in knowing that his love to me is utterly realistic, based at every point on prior knowledge about me, so that no discovery now can disillusion him about me, in the way that I am so often disillusioned about myself."[13] I remember when I read Packer's words for the first time while sitting in my dorm room at the University of Michigan, struggling with my own guilt about sexual sin. I longed for purity, and Packer described exactly how I felt: disillusioned with myself in my stumbling walk. In my shame, I wanted to hide from God. Knowing that God could see me—in all my mess—and still love me was incredible. When we try to hide from God, we lose out on the amazing gift of God's forgiveness and re-demptive power. That forgiveness should move us, as it did David in Psalm 103:2-5, 10-12:

> Praise the Lord, my soul;
>   and forget not all his benefits—
> who forgives all your sins
>   and heals all your diseases,
> who redeems your life from the pit
>   and crowns you with love and compassion,
> who satisfies your desires with good things
>   so that your youth is renewed like the eagle's. . . .
> He does not treat us as our sins deserve
>   or repay us according to our iniquities.
> For as high as the heavens are above the earth,
>   so great is his love for those who fear him;
> as far as the east is from the west,
>   so far has he removed our transgressions from us.

When we have sinned sexually, we can feel lost in a pit of despair and brokenness. Yet our hope is in this God: the God who forgives *all* our

---

[13]J. I. Packer, *Knowing God* (Downers Grove, Ill.: InterVarsity Press, 1973), p. 42.

sins and redeems our lives from the pit. Believe in the promise of God, that our sins are removed as far as the east is from the west. Redeemed sexuality is forgiven sexuality—and leads to restored sexuality.

SINGLE SEXUALITY

At its core, sexuality is about the pursuit of intimacy. Lewis Smedes writes, "Sexuality is the human drive toward intimate communion."[14] We are created in the image of God, and as such, we have been made sexual beings with a deep longing for connection. However, as theologian Stanley Grenz points out, it is not only—or even primarily—through the sexual union in marriage that we reflect God's image as people-in-relationship. Rather, our sexuality is one more reminder that we are not made for this world, that God is preparing us to be his bride: "Although marriage is the primal male-female relationship, the biblical narrative points to the eschatological new creation as the fullness of fellowship toward which human sexuality has been directed from the beginning. For this reason, the image of God is not present solely, or even primarily, in the marital union."[15] In other words, the image of God is best represented not by the marital relationship but by the body of Christ—the church.

We are sexual beings because we are relational beings, but sex is not required to experience relational intimacy. Jesus is the perfect image of God, and he remained single and celibate. How can sexual union be the primary path to relational intimacy if our own Lord chose not to engage in it? If we argue that this is because of his deity, we devalue his humanity. God created us as inescapably relational beings with a deep longing for connection, but this intimacy need not be romantic or sexual to be fulfilling:

> Once we have discovered essentially who we are, we long to share that self in an intimate relationship with another. For many people

---

[14]Smedes, *Sex for Christians*, p. 32.
[15]Stanley Grenz, *The Social God and the Relational Self: A Trinitarian Theology of the Imago Dei* (Louisville, Ky.: Westminster John Knox Press, 2001), p. 302.

this intimate relationship is marriage. Yet this is not automatic. Many marriages know no bonds of intimacy beyond physical coupling, while many single persons, aside from sexual union, have found the deepest sharing within friendship.[16]

Our sexuality urges us to bond with others. Smedes argues that although sexual union is not *the* superior avenue for expressing the drive toward connection, it is the most common one. He suggests that singles can express the relational drive "by giving themselves to other persons without physical sex. Through a life of self-giving—which is at the heart of sexual union—they become whole persons."[17]

This attitude toward single sexuality, that singles can express their sexuality through "self-giving" and intimate friendship, makes sense to me intellectually. However, when a woman comes to me who is not at peace with singleness as a chosen vocation but is single because she has not found a longed-for life partner or because she is widowed or divorced, I fear offering theological answers. I am not walking in her place, and I do not want to silence my single clients' and friends' real questions and frustrations.

Jane, a woman in her late thirties who came to me for counseling a few years ago, was confident, smart and witty. She loved her job and had many interesting hobbies. Jane had not dated anyone in several years. Although people have differing opinions on whether God calls us to either marriage or singleness, Jane was beginning to believe God had called her to be single. Yet Jane longed to have someone to share life with, raise children with—a companion and lover. When she saw her friends staying at home with their children, it tapped into her sadness regarding her unmet desire to be a mother. It was also a harsh reminder that her friends were going through life with a partner. Jane longed for that kind of companionship and intimacy, but instead, she felt like she

---

[16]Letha Dawn Scanzoni and Nancy A. Hardesty, *All We're Meant to Be: Biblical Feminism for Today*, 3rd ed. (Grand Rapids: Eerdmans, 1992), p. 256.
[17]Smedes, *Sex for Christians*, p. 34.

was doing life on her own. Jane wistfully talked about the quiet comfort in having someone to come home to, but she also discussed the practical challenges of single living. While her friends shared household tasks with their husbands, Jane maintained a full-time job and still did all the cooking, cleaning, shopping, yard work and home repairs. To make matters worse, Jane's sexual drive had been climbing in recent years. But where could she put those impulses? She did not believe in sex outside of marriage, but she did not see marriage in her future.

Jane is not alone in her longing for intimacy, both physical and relational, as a single woman. Consider the words of another single woman, who participated in a large study on female sexuality:

> Personally, as a single person it is difficult to come to terms with my own desires and the inability to explore those with a partner. Although I believe it is possible to live without being sexually active, I so much want to believe God intends it for everyone. Sex in a fallen world is a mystery still for many of us.[18]

This woman and Jane both reflect how frustrating and confusing it can be to cope with sexual impulses and desires as a single woman. I wish I had a theologically profound and personally meaningful response for single women who have God-given sexual feelings and no outlet, but I do not. Clearly, it is true that we can express the longing for connection through nonsexual intimate relationships. But what to do with sexual feelings?

Susan Annette Muto, a spiritual writer and single woman, suggests that when we become single through circumstances like death or divorce this can urge us toward God: "When life as one knows it falls apart, one can ask the faith question: 'What is God trying to tell me?' "[19] As Jane and I worked together, this is the question we explored. Although her life had not fallen apart through the loss of a husband, she had lost the dream of a husband. In our counseling relationship, we grieved that loss.

---

[18]Anonymous participant quoted in Archibold Hart, Catherine Hart Weber and Debra Taylor, *Secrets of Eve* (Nashville: Word, 1998), p. 201.
[19]Muto, *Celebrating the Single Life,* pp. 58-59.

Of course, Jane's single status could change, but Jane came to me in large part because she believed God was calling her to the single life. Even as she pursued that calling, we mourned her unmet hopes and desires for romantic love—both emotional and physical. I did not tell Jane she should be happy with the many gifts God had given her, although her life was indeed filled with good things. I did not suggest that Jane be content in all things, although I believe in the truth of Philippians 4:12, that it is possible to be content in any situation.[20] I did not pretend to understand her experience, because that would be dishonest and fake. I had no idea what life had been like for Jane. Instead, I tried to be present to Jane in her pain and fear and sadness.

As Jane and I walked together, she taught me about finding peace in the midst of disappointment, about finding wholeness in brokenness, and about finding love and passion in unexpected places. As Muto writes, "Being single offers one an opportunity to celebrate life in a new way. One can focus on the limits of this condition, but it is more creative to discover its unique possibilities."[21] Jane renewed my firm belief that there are no easy answers and that real intimacy is found in a community of genuineness and honesty. Although Jane was not living the life she would have imagined, Jane taught me about being surprised by grace—because somehow, in a way that was previously unimaginable to her, Jane began to find joy in her journey and to celebrate her singleness.

TOOLS FOR THE JOURNEY

Grieve your losses. Our sexuality can be a source of joy and pleasure, but it can also be a place of disappointment and loss. Some have been sexually violated. Others are living lives of celibacy and have no opportunity to physically express their sexuality despite their sexual nature and urges. Still others are involved in sexually intimate relationships that

---

[20]"I know what it is to be in need, and I know what it is to have plenty. I have learned the secret of being content in any and every situation, whether well fed or hungry, whether living in plenty or in want."

[21]Muto, *Celebrating the Single Life,* pp. 62-63.

are painful or disappointing. In order to grow in wholeness, grieving whatever loss you've experienced is an important step.

If you have been sexually violated in some way, you have experienced loss. If you were sexually abused as a child, you lost the opportunity to enter the world of sexuality by choice, at a time when you were emotionally and physically ready. You lost the chance to choose who you would experience sexuality with for the first time. You lost the innocence and vulnerability of a child. You may have lost the ability to trust men or to experience sex without guilt or pain. Your losses are unique to you and your story, but an essential aspect of healing is naming and grieving those losses.

If you are a single woman who longs for an intimate relationship with a partner, for sexual closeness as well as physical companionship, you have experienced loss. When your hopes for your future have been thwarted and your dreams of life with a trusted other have not come true, you may feel betrayed or disappointed. If you long to express your sexual desires toward another person and enjoy the pleasure of sexual intimacy, the pain of being alone may be overwhelming. If these things are true of your experience, then you too need to grieve your losses.

If you are a married woman whose sexual relationship has been unfulfilling, perhaps even painful, then you also need to grieve your losses. Perhaps you waited until marriage to have sex for the first time, but now your sexual relationship is painful or stale. You do not experience pleasure, and you cannot escape the guilt or dirty feelings you learned about sex as a girl. You see unmarried sex portrayed as ecstatic in movies and television, and you wonder why your dreams of sexual fulfillment have been shattered. You did the right thing, and yet your sexual relationship is far from the stuff of fantasies. You, too, need to grieve the loss that your actual sexual relationship is not meeting your expectations or dreams.

Perhaps your losses have to do with a husband's betrayal or insensitivity. Although you long to trust your husband and build a safe and intimate relationship, both physically and emotionally, your hopes have been lost through a husband's secret sexual life. You, too, need to grieve for the loss of trust and safety in your relationship, as well as the personal losses you have suffered through your husband's betrayal.

Or maybe you need to grieve the loss of sexual purity—even if it was not taken from you but freely given. Perhaps you are stuck in guilt over your sexual sin, and you need to lay your guilt at Christ's feet. Remember that your past is not your lord—Christ is Lord, and he has saved and redeemed you. Your past does not determine who you are or who you are becoming—Christ does. So grieve the past and ask God to help you let it go, for you are a new creation in Christ. Even in the area of sexuality, experiencing Christ's restoration and renewal is possible. Even though it may take some time to fully receive it, he will not give up on you no matter how long it takes.

Naming and grieving your losses does not change the past. It does not magically make things better. But it can change you. And in beginning the process of inward change, you can grow toward healing and wholeness.

Get educated. Many women who struggle with low sex drive, pain during intercourse, or an inability to experience sexual pleasure or orgasm lack a basic understanding of sexuality. Sex, to some degree, is a biological phenomenon made up of four phases: excitement, plateau, orgasm and resolution. Physical changes coincide with each of these phases in both men and women. Understanding those physiological changes and how they are different for men and women can help you make sense of your own sexual experience. Gaining an explicit understanding of both male and female anatomy and erogenous zones can provide helpful information about how you and your husband can give each other sexual pleasure. Many of the women I see in counseling do not even talk about their sexual organs, much less possess an intricate understanding of what they look like, how they are stimulated or how they reach orgasm. Movies portray sex as a raw and ecstatic experience, and it certainly can be, but it does not happen magically. Getting educated about sex and your own body does not take the romance out of physical intimacy. Rather, it increases the likelihood that you and your partner will be able to experience greater pleasure and intimacy.

Sex education is not something you need to do alone. Your sexual relationship with your husband is not your responsibility; it is a joint responsibility between you and your husband. Getting educated is something you can do together. If one of you is experiencing pain or disinterest, both partners must be proactive to create a safe sexual environment that will allow for clear, open communication, growth and healing. If this seems threatening, I would encourage you to reflect on and perhaps talk to a counselor about some of the deeper issues in your marriage. Reading a good book on sexuality together can help you address some of the marital issues that could be interfering with your sexual intimacy. Doug Rosenau's book *A Celebration of Sex* is an excellent place to start.[22] Rosenau is an expert in sex therapy and provides accurate education as well as practical exercises and interventions.

For example, if you want to experience good sex, you must first think good sex thoughts. Rosenau suggests, "Sex is perhaps 80 percent fantasy (imagination and mind) and about 20 percent friction."[23] Therefore, if you want to improve your sexual desire and enjoyment, you have to change the way you think about sex. If you tell yourself that sex is dirty and disgusting, then you are not going to want sex or enjoy it. If, instead, you tell yourself that sex is beautiful and erotic, then you are going to be more interested. Think about having sex with your husband. Wear underwear that helps you feel sexy. Set the mood. Play sensual music. Light candles. Fantasize about good experiences with your husband.

If even the thought of reading about sex and your own body makes you uncomfortable, take some time to review the negative messages you may have internalized about sexuality. Make a list of the things you learned about sex and your own body as a child. Be honest and do not edit your list. Write about the things you picked up, in overt and subtle ways, from movies and television, teachers and classmates, parents and siblings. Then review your list and challenge the harmful and degrading

---

[22]Doug Rosenau, *A Celebration of Sex: A Guide to Enjoying God's Gift of Sexual Intimacy* (Nashville: Thomas Nelson, 1994).

[23]Ibid., p. 86.

messages. Dispute those messages with healthier and more truthful statements. Remind yourself that God made you in his image as a sexual creature, and sex is designed for pleasure. Read Song of Songs in the Old Testament, and reflect on what you can learn about a God who includes this kind of erotic love poem in his Word.

Invite God into the bedroom. God created our sexuality and sex to be beautiful and good, but that beauty has been perverted in our culture. Bring your fear and shame, your sin and questions, into the light. Present your sexuality to God, and ask for his healing touch. If you are married and struggling in your sexual relationship, ask God before and even during physically intimate moments to help you relax and honor him with your actions. Present your unique requests and needs before God. Rather than hide from him, walk openly into his loving embrace. You might pray something like this: "God, help me to relax so I can enjoy this time with my husband. Help me to be unashamed of the body you have given me and this act of sexual union that you designed. Help me to be free and spontaneous. Give me a spirit of joy and fun." The words you choose do not matter, but bring your sexuality and sex before the Lord and ask that he would enable you to accept them as gifts.

Many of us feel so ashamed of our own sexuality or the sexual act that we try to hide our sexual nature from God. Others of us are weighed down by guilt from sexual sin, yet as Bruce Narramore points out in his book *No Condemnation,* "the word *guilt* is never used as an emotion in the New Testament," and "Christians are *never* commanded to feel guilty."[24] God calls us to purity and life change, not to get stuck in guilt—which often keeps us from change. If the thought of God looking down on you in your most sexually vulnerable moments fills you with shame and guilt, then bring those feelings before God. You are a sexual being because God chose to create you that way, and your sexual relationship is an expression and reflection of his divine love. When you try

---

[24]Bruce Narramore, *No Condemnation: Rethinking Guilt Motivation in Counseling, Preaching, and Parenting* (Grand Rapids: Academie Books, 1984), p. 291.

to hide your nakedness and sexuality from God, you end up replaying the Garden of Eden drama. Yet Christ came to reverse that drama so you would not need to be ashamed. We cannot hope for healing if we do not bring that which is broken before our Healer.

By talking with God about your journey toward wholeness and healing, you invite him to show you the way. Although God promises his presence to us, we sometimes forget he is there. Perhaps we don't see him or even look for him. We may not feel his presence in the way we would like, but even when there is no material evidence for it, prayer reorients us to the divine presence in our lives.

Life is not divided into the secular and the sacred—*all* of life is sacred. God is with us all the time. As the proverb states, "Bidden or not bidden, God is present." God is not present only when we are in church, having religious discussions or listening to Christian music. Rather, when we are fighting with our sisters, getting our hair done or being sexually intimate with our husbands, God is present. Sexuality is not something to hide from God. Rather, sex was created by God, and it is essential to our personhood. Although that essence has been distorted, Christ came to earth to reverse the effects of the Fall. Therefore, embrace your sexuality as the gift that it is, and allow God to be present in it.

9

The Search for Connection

GROWING HEALTHY INTIMATE RELATIONSHIPS

The Christian spiritual journey is a journey we take with others.

Each of us must take our own journey,

and for each of us that journey will be unique.

But none of us is intended to make that journey alone.

DAVID BENNER
SACRED COMPANIONS:
THE GIFT OF SPIRITUAL FRIENDSHIP & DIRECTION

Intimacy means that we can be who we are in a relationship,

and allow the other person to do the same.

HARRIET GOLDHOR LERNER
THE DANCE OF INTIMACY: A WOMAN'S GUIDE TO
COURAGEOUS ACTS OF CHANGE IN KEY RELATIONSHIPS

My husband dreads picking out movie rentals with me. "What about this one?" he'll ask hopefully, lifting up a DVD with a sweaty soldier climbing out of a tank, a machine gun strapped to his back. "Do people shoot each other more than they talk to each other in it?" I ask him. He sighs and puts the movie back, longingly gazing at the action and adventure section.

While my husband and I love engaging in friendly banter over which movies to watch, my question about talking versus shooting is really another way of asking him if the movie has a significant relational dimension. I love movies about relationships, and not just romantic ones. My husband and I both actually love relational movies (he just enjoys those in a war setting more than I do). We love stories about the common struggle to know and be known in relationships between mothers and daughters, fathers and sons, friends, neighbors and siblings. When I review the popularity of relational movies, books, songs and television shows, it's clear that we are not alone.

People care about relationships, and rightly so. We are created in the image of God, and as such, we are relational beings. As I have already discussed, some theologians suggest that we reflect God primarily in the context of relationships: "Only in fellowship with others can we show forth what God is like, for God is the community of love—the eternal relationship between the Father, Son and Holy Spirit."[1] We long for healthy, whole relationships, and not just with spouses or boyfriends. We want to feel connected to our mothers and daughters, our sisters and friends. It is precisely in these intimate relationships that we image God best. Although we long to feel a deep sense of knowing and being known by those we care about, we often feel like this kind of intimacy is missing in our relationships.

In our longing for healthy and whole relationships, some of us become so intent on finding intimacy that we will do anything to maintain relationships, even if we lose our very selves in the process. Others of us value relationships so much that we want them to be perfect, and we create unrealistic expectations for others—not allowing others to be who

---

[1]Stanley J. Grenz and Denise Muir Kjesbo, *Women in the Church: A Biblical Theology of Women in Ministry* (Downers Grove, Ill.: Inter Varsity Press, 1995), p. 171.

they really are. Mary Stewart Van Leeuwen refers to this distortion of our natural longing for intimate relationships as social enmeshment, and she suggests that it is one of the consequences of the Fall.[2] After the introduction of sin into our world, women are warned in Genesis 3:16, "Your desire will be for your husband." Although both males and females are called to exercise accountable dominion (fill the earth and subdue it), Van Leeuwen argues that the Fall led to gendered distortions of that mandate: "The first (the man's sin) is to try to exercise dominion without regard for God's original plan for male/female relationships. But the second—the peculiarly female sin—is to use the preservation of those relationships as an excuse not to exercise accountable dominion in the first place."[3] As creatures accountable to God for his creation, we are responsible for managing the gifts God has given us, and one of those gifts is ourselves. When we restrict, ignore or suppress certain aspects of ourselves in order to hold on to relationships with others, we are not being good stewards of the gifts God has entrusted to us. Likewise, when we insist that others act in particular ways to meet our relational needs, we are not respecting their gifts.

In this chapter I will explore the consequences of this social enmeshment and some of the common struggles women encounter in relationships. Sometimes when we hear people talk about intimate relationships, we immediately assume they mean romantic or marriage relationships. Intimacy, however, is not restricted to the bedroom, and we lose out on many sources of closeness if we only look for connection through romantic relationships. In this chapter I will examine skills for going deeper in relationships with all kinds of significant others: friends and sisters, parents and spouses. In order to grow healthy and intimate relationships, we must interact as whole people, not shutting off parts of ourselves or pretending to be someone we are not. In addition, we must invite others to be whole people as well, not demanding or expecting them to be ex-

---

[2]Mary Stuart Van Leeuwen, *Gender & Grace: Love, Work & Parenting in a Changing World* (Downers Grove, Ill.: InterVarsity Press, 1990), p. 46.
[3]Ibid., pp. 45-46.

actly what we want or need, but seeing them as the unique people God created. Whole relationships require that *we* learn to be authentic in relationships, and that we allow and invite *others* to be real and genuine with us.

GETTING REAL IN RELATIONSHIPS

Jenny, a thirty-three-year-old single woman I saw in counseling for an eating disorder, is an example of a woman who longed for the kind of intimacy that can be found in close relationships. As a child, Jenny had experienced a variety of relational wounds; as an adolescent and adult, Jenny struggled to keep her eating disorder a secret. Consequently, Jenny felt isolated and alone. She didn't like to spend too much time with her family because they were proud of her and thought she was the "perfect daughter." She hated to think how disappointed they would be if they knew that, for example, when she left the dinner table, she was secretly purging in the bathroom. With friends, Jenny was always worrying they were watching her shift the food around on her plate. She felt like an imposter and worried that her friends mainly spent time with her because they felt sorry for her. Some of her friends were married, and others seemed closer to each other than to her. Jenny constantly felt like a third wheel. She felt disconnected from her family, her friends and herself, yet she desperately wanted to feel loved and cared for. Although Jenny's experience is rooted in her unique battle with an eating disorder, her struggle is one that many women can relate to: an intense desire to feel that others love us, even when we are struggling to love ourselves.

David Benner writes, "The deep knowing of both self and God foundational to Christian spirituality demands deep knowing of and being known by others."[4] Jenny, like most women, longed for this kind of deep knowing with others, but she tended to skip over the knowing of self. As discussed in chapter seven, we cannot offer the gift of ourselves in rela-

---

[4]David Benner, *Sacred Companions: The Gift of Spiritual Friendship and Direction* (Downers Grove, Ill.: InterVarsity Press, 2002), p. 41.

tionships with others if we don't even know who that self is! Therefore, the first task for building healthy relationships is getting to know yourself. Healthy relationships begin with people who know and respect themselves. Before Jenny could be honest with others about who she was and her struggles, she first had to get honest with herself. For Jenny, that involved professional counseling and, ultimately, completing an intensive treatment program for her eating disorder. Over the course of counseling, Jenny learned that she would never find true intimacy with another unless she first became intimate with herself, exploring her likes and dislikes, as well as her deeper fears and dreams, regrets and wounds. Brennan Manning writes, "Experience has taught me that I connect best with others when I connect with the core of myself."[5] By looking inward, Jenny was better prepared to reach outward to connect with significant others.

Healthy and intimate relationships require not only that we *know* who we are but that we *share* who we are with others. Sometimes that means sharing our inner thoughts and opinions instead of going along with others or pretending to be someone we're not. Sometimes it means being vulnerable and sharing our hurt and pain. So often, however, we do not share our authentic selves with others; we hide our real selves instead. Perhaps we cover our insecurity and fear with overstated confidence, with alcohol or other substances, or with joking and laughter. As theologian T. F. Torrance writes, "The image we present, and wish to present, to others has become detached from what we actually are, so that it becomes a deceptive mask."[6] These masks keep us from real relationships with others.

Letting go of our masks, however, requires courage. Our fear of rejection or hurt can be overwhelming at times: "We believe if we were truly known we would not be loved. Many of us in our heart of hearts believe this: if that close friend could really see into my soul, she would see me for who I really am and no longer like me. We believe that to be known

---

[5]Brennan Manning, *Abba's Child: The Cry of the Heart for Intimate Belonging* (Colorado Springs: NavPress, 1994), p. 56.
[6]T. F. Torrance, *The Mediation of Christ* (Grand Rapids: Eerdmans, 1983), p. 79.

means not to be loved."[7] Although our fear of being misunderstood, ignored or minimized can be paralyzing, we will never experience the joy of community and connection if we don't take risks and share our real selves with others.

Of course, people may not always respond with acceptance, affirmation or support when we are vulnerable and share ourselves with them. But intimacy begins with us, and we can only control who *we* are in a relationship. If we want to experience greater intimacy, we have to offer more of ourselves. Psychologist David Schnarch suggests that intimacy involves taking an honest look at ourselves and sharing that self with our partners. He differentiates between *other*-validated intimacy and *self*-validated intimacy. In other-validated intimacy, we disclose things about ourselves to our partners with the expectation that the other person will be empathic, validating and equally disclosing. This is the kind of intimacy in which we expect others to tell us who we are and make us feel okay about ourselves. As discussed in chapter six, this kind of demand places others in a god-role that they cannot and should not fill. Schnarch contrasts this with *self*-validated intimacy, in which we share ourselves with our partners without expectation of acceptance or validation. Some psychologists refer to this ability to maintain our sense of worth and identity in relationships as differentiation. Self-validated intimacy or differentiation looks something like this:

> *I don't expect you to agree with me; you weren't put on the face of the earth to validate and reinforce me. But I want you to love me—and you can't really do that if you don't know me. I don't want your rejection—but I must face that possibility if I'm ever to feel accepted or secure with you.*[8]

In self-validated intimacy, we do not rely on our partners to make us feel

---

[7]Mary Ellen Ashcroft, *Balancing Act: How Women Can Lose Their Roles and Find Their Callings* (Downers Grove, Ill.: InterVarsity Press, 1996), p. 86.

[8]David Schnarch, *Passionate Marriage: Keeping Love and Intimacy Alive in Committed Relationships* (New York: Owl Books, 1997), p. 107.

okay, but instead, we depend on our own sense of self-worth and identity.

Although this distinction between self- and other-validated intimacy is helpful, an even better option is *Christ*-validated intimacy. If I rely only on myself for my sense of security and comfort, I am destined to feel inadequate because I mess up and fall down over and over again. It would be natural for me to then look to my husband or my friends to make me feel better about myself. If we have to depend solely on ourselves for our sense of identity, it is no wonder that we turn to others to make us feel okay! We are imperfect, fallen people. Yet we have a better option—a much better option. As Jack and Judy Balswick write, "Being dependent on Christ alleviates an overdemanding concentration on the spouse [or others] to meet our needs."[9] Instead, we can look to Christ and find our security, peace and identity in him. Because we are complete in Christ, we need not look to others to make us feel complete or okay. With that solid foundation, we are freed to see others for who they really are, instead of who we wish or need them to be for us. Christ came to restore us in every way—including our ability to form authentic relationships with others. Although we hide and posture and pretend in order to protect ourselves, Christ lived a life of perfect authenticity. Our fear of rejection can be disabling, but through holding onto the work Christ has already done to redeem us from our sin and imperfection, we can find courage to let go of our own masks and get real with people.

Jenny took a risk by coming to see me for counseling. She had never talked to anyone about her eating disorder and all those factors that led up to it. Although she was fearful, Jenny didn't feel like she could carry her burden alone anymore. She knew she needed help and support, and so she took a great risk by sharing her story with me. "Community arises where the sharing of pain takes place," Henri Nouwen writes.[10] When Jenny shared her story with me, we found this kind of community together. I listened to Jenny's story and I asked questions. At particularly

---

[9]Jack O. Balswick and Judith K. Balswick, *A Model for Marriage: Covenant, Grace, Empowerment and Intimacy* (Downers Grove, Ill.: InterVarsity Press, 2006), p. 97.
[10]Henri Nouwen, *The Wounded Healer* (New York: Doubleday, 1972), p. 94.

poignant moments, my eyes filled with tears as Jenny described her hurt and shame. Even though it was scary for her, Jenny later told me that sharing her real self was worth the risk. Jenny felt like a burden had been lifted because she could stop trying to pretend she had everything together. Even though she feared rejection and judgment, she knew that by sharing herself with me up front that I would not find out the truth later and be disappointed, shocked or horrified. Although Jenny feared I would think she was shameful and dirty, when Jenny opened up to me, I saw a beautiful, hurting child of God. We connected, and I'm grateful to this day that Jenny took that risk with me.

In addition to knowing ourselves and sharing that self in relationship, we also grow in wholeness when we cultivate *direct* relationships. When we get wounded in relationships, even when it is unintentional, it is tempting to alleviate our pain by talking about our hurt feelings, anger or frustration with someone other than the person who caused it. Psychologists refer to this indirect relational pain management technique as *triangulation* because, instead of dealing with the person directly, we create a triangle between the person who hurt us, ourselves and another person.

For example, Jenny's younger sister, Kate, had a caustic sense of humor that sometimes deeply hurt Jenny. During the course of our work together, Jenny spoke about her deep desire to share her struggle with Kate, but she feared that her disclosure would somehow become the object of Kate's biting wit. Instead of speaking directly to Kate, Jenny would sometimes try to work out her own internal anxiety and frustration about her sister's thoughtlessness by talking about Kate with her older brother, Jack. When Jack agreed with her and provided additional examples of Kate's hurtful comments, this only served to increase Jenny's frustration. It did not help her develop a closer relationship with Kate, because Kate never knew what she had done to hurt Jenny, and consequently, she could not repair it.

Although Jenny felt more connected to Jack after talking about their shared frustrations, it was really a false intimacy based on mutual complaints or criticisms of a third party—rather than shared interests, care and respect. When someone hurts, angers or offends us, the reason we often pull another person in is to release the tension that those negative emotions raise for us. But developing healthy and whole relationships requires courage. Even though it is scary and puts us in a vulnerable position, we need to deal with hurts directly. Instead of talking to Jack about Kate, Jenny needed to take the risk of talking to Kate herself. Only by giving Kate direct feedback could she and Kate experience greater intimacy.

Triangulation is not the only way we try to manage our hurt feelings. Sometimes we make passive-aggressive jokes or comments. Other times, we say nothing to the offending party, but we let our resentment build into bitterness. We may then unwittingly punish the other person by shutting them out. Not only did Jenny talk to Jack about Kate, but she sometimes wouldn't answer her phone when Kate called, and she often tried to avoid Kate at family gatherings.

However, relationships should be a source of growth, so bless people by being honest and clear when they have hurt you. This is a difficult task because you have to acknowledge your own vulnerability. Sharing that hurt, however, could be the doorway that allows you to go to new depths in your relationship.

Jenny took the risk to move away from what was comfortable—shutting Kate out and talking about her with Jack—and began sharing her feelings directly with Kate. Jenny told Kate that she loved her and wanted to be close, but she feared opening up to her, because she feared Kate would minimize her pain by poking fun at her. Although Kate was defensive at first, she ultimately heard Jenny's genuine desire for closeness. Kate looked up to Jenny and told her that she sometimes tried to impress Jenny with her jokes. She even admitted to feeling jealous of Jenny, who did everything first and whom everyone seemed to love. Jenny's decision to take a risk and share her hurt with Kate led to a two-hour conversation in which Kate and Jenny talked openly about their childhood, their parents and their fears about the future. Although there is no guarantee that taking risks like Jenny did will lead to greater connection, we are guaranteed to have shallow relationships that lack depth and intimacy if we choose *not* to take risks.

ALLOWING OTHERS TO BE REAL

Not only do we need to treat ourselves as whole people in order to cultivate healthy and whole relationships, but we must also allow and invite others to be whole people. When Jerry Maguire told Dorothy, "You complete me," he revealed a cultural myth that many of us buy into—that someone else can make us whole. But this is an illusion, and it is the first thing we must let go of if we want to find true intimacy. No human being can tell us who we are or mirror us perfectly. No other person can make us feel whole, okay, adequate or fulfilled. Likewise, we cannot save or complete anyone else. When we try to save someone, or we expect the other person to save us, we will never experience the joy of true intimacy.

We allow others to be who they really are when we respect them as separate from us. Intimate relationships are not like lattes, where the coffee and milk are blended so well that you are unable to identify where one ends and the other begins. Rather, they are more like cappuccinos, where you can clearly taste and even see the difference between the coffee mixture and the frothy foam on top. There is unity (one drink) but also diversity (different taste and texture). Real relationships involve two distinct persons who have made a choice to come together. "It is the distinction (differentiation) rather than fusion (dependency) that leads to vital connection and wholeness."[11] An intimate relationship celebrates and protects the differences and the boundaries between persons.

Some of the women I talk to feel confused about what it means to remain as two separate people in light of the Bible's teaching on marriage. Didn't Jesus tell us that we "are no longer two, but one"(Matthew 19:6)? Yes! We are called to be one with our spouse in marriage, but this oneness celebrates differences; it does not ignore or erase them. It is similar to the oneness that God experiences within the Trinity—unity in diversity:

---

[11]Balswick and Balswick, *Model for Marriage,* p. 33.

Following the pattern of the trinitarian relationships, such relationships are characterized by mutuality, give and take, and they enable the self to be known most fully in the process of knowing another. In such relationships there is space to simultaneously be oneself and to be in relationship with each other. There is room to encounter the other and to encounter the self through the other. The self is never lost in face of the other.[12]

Whole relationships are reciprocal relationships in which we allow others to be themselves. Theologian Stanley Grenz puts it this way: "the unity in diversity that arises out of the bond that brings male and female together in marriage offers an obvious picture of the unity in diversity present within the triune God."[13] We do not lose ourselves in another person; rather, we understand where we end and the other person begins, and we do not try to ignore or erase those lines.

When we view others as separate people and give up the illusion that we can save each other, we are freed to see the other people for who they really are, instead of as who we wish them to be. Sometimes we hold a fantasy of the perfect friend or husband in our minds, and the real friend or husband is not as strong, thoughtful, affectionate, confident, brave, decisive and so on as in our fantasy. As Schnarch points out, many people would "rather make love to the fantasy in their head than the partner in their bed."[14] When the real people in our lives don't live up to our unrealistic expectations, we are disappointed. We have made the mistake of viewing them through the lens of who we think they should be to fulfill our fantasy, instead of who God has created them to be. Consequently, we may try to make decisions for them or control their choices and opinions, molding them into the people we wish they were, instead of respecting and valuing the unique creatures they already are.

---

[12]Jack O. Balswick, Pamela Ebstyne King and Kevin Reimer, *The Reciprocating Self: Human Development in Theological Perspective* (Downers Grove, Ill.: InterVarsity Press, 2005), p. 36.

[13]Stanley Grenz, *The Social God and the Relational Self: A Trinitarian Theology of the Imago Dei* (Louisville, Ky.: Westminster John Knox Press, 2001), p. 302.

[14]Schnarch, *Passionate Marriage,* p. 188.

I sometimes view my husband through this lens of who I think he should be, and it usually looks like this: he should do things like me, feel like me and think like me. From loading the dishwasher to mapping out a trip to caring for our son, I sometimes get frustrated when Jeff's way is not my way. And every time I fall into this trap, I miss out on the joy of interacting with my husband's real self. When we try to control the people we care about, we miss out on the joy of differences. God has created us differently, and regardless of how strongly we may believe it, none of us have the market on the "right" way to do things. When we let those we care about express themselves and do things their own way, especially when it is markedly different from our way of doing things, we speak love in our actions. Sometimes people will make mistakes, of course, and when we value them as separate people, we want to protect and cherish their selfhood, meaning that we won't demean them by pointing out their weaknesses or mistakes simply because they have done things differently than we would have.

When we stop insisting that others meet our need to save or protect, or to be saved or protected, then we can cease our subtle efforts to change or fix the other person. In the process, we can discover a wonderful gift—the gift of the other person's true self. We are then freed to experience and learn from other people's gifts. For me, a special gift resulted when I allowed Jeff to be himself in our marriage: he helped me become more flexible and spontaneous, qualities that have helped me to enjoy my life and my family.

When we see others as separate people and allow them to be who they are, we can then appreciate their unique gifts and personalities, rather than view those differences as threats. Being able to celebrate differences is particularly important for female relationships. Competition between females is a timeless problem, and the media depicts this competition in vivid ways. For example, consider how many times you have seen gossiping or backstabbing females in television shows or movies. Perhaps those women are fighting each other for a man's romantic affection. Or perhaps the women in conflict are family members. They might be sisters competing for a parent's affection or a mother-in-law trying to woo her son's loyalty away from his wife. If we watch daytime soap operas, female competition gets even nastier and more dangerous. The media portrays women as posing a threat to each other, and many women struggle with this in their own lives. Kathleen Fischer describes one woman's struggle to be in a group with other women: "Her first response was to see herself in competition with them, and she was embarrassed to have to admit that she did not really think she liked women."[15] We will not make progress on our own journey toward wholeness if we do not learn to become cheerleaders and sisters for other women who are sharing our journey.

If you struggle with seeing women as competitors—whether the woman you are competing with is your beautiful neighbor, your critical mother, your eloquent Bible study leader, your husband's talented sister or mother, or your son's assertive wife—practice reframing your thoughts. Remind yourself that God has created that woman in his own image with special gifts and skills. The fact that she has these gifts is not a criticism toward you, but it is how God has uniquely expressed himself through her. Remind yourself that she is a reflection of your Creator.

Of course, appreciating differences is helpful not only in female relationships. By seeing the hand of the Creator in the diversity of people's gifts, preferences and opinions, this also allows us to view disagreements or challenges in a new way. We can genuinely invite others to be honest with us, even when that means telling us they disagree with our opinions or decisions, or telling us when we have hurt or offended them. We can learn to view confrontations and disagreements as a gift, because they indicate that others trust us enough to be honest, and they provide an opportunity to grow through that struggle and develop greater intimacy. When someone disagrees with us, challenges our opinions or decisions, or confronts us with a way in which we have hurt or offended them, it

---

[15]Kathleen Fischer, *Women at the Well: Feminist Perspectives on Spiritual Direction* (New York: Paulist, 1988), p. 204.

is tempting to get defensive. Real relationships, however, are cultivated when we consider others' opinions or feedback, take responsibility for how we have hurt or offended them, and intentionally seek ways to repair and grow deeper. If we truly want to grow intimate relationships, we need to begin to see disagreements and challenges as opportunities for growth and as ways to build stronger connections.

Learning to be grateful for disagreements and challenges, however, is not easy. When Jenny decided to seek counseling and take medication for her eating disorder and underlying depression, she was challenged by Anne, a friend from church who had been taught that depression was solely a spiritual battle. For Jenny to take the risk to share her struggle and her decision with Anne was significant, because Jenny was tempted to isolate herself and shut Anne out when Anne disclosed her differing views. But Jenny had begun to experience the beauty of intimacy in a few select relationships, and so she decided to invite Anne to be a whole person, even when that meant she didn't see things in the same way as Jenny. Jenny reminded herself that just because Anne didn't agree with Jenny's decision didn't mean that Anne disliked *her*. Jenny reframed her automatic thought that Anne disagreeing with her was a personal attack into an opportunity to have an interesting and revealing conversation— not one in which Jenny tried to *change* Anne, but one in which Jenny *got to know her better*. Jenny discovered that Anne had struggled with postpartum depression and that Anne's husband had wanted her to take antidepressants. Anne felt like her husband wanted her to take pills as a quick fix so that she would just get better and he wouldn't have to deal with her sadness anymore. For Anne, the decision not to take medication was a difficult one, and she felt constantly criticized for it by her husband. Because Jenny did not respond defensively, she was blessed by a very real conversation in which Anne shared her story. That talk marked the beginning of a new kind of connection between Jenny and Anne. Anne came to realize that Jenny's decision was the right one for her, and she became an ardent supporter of Jenny's struggle to stay healthy with the help of counseling and medication, even though she chose not to take medication for her own struggle. Jenny would never have experienced this kind of intimacy with Anne, however, if she had not invited Anne to be fully herself—even when that meant disagreeing with or challenging Jenny.

We can foster whole relationships by allowing others to be real with us, respecting boundaries and differences, but we can go one step further. We cultivate whole relationships when we choose to be vulnerable and use our voice to speak the truth in love—not only when that truth is sharing hurt and pain but also when that truth is sharing affirmation and blessing. In 1 Thessalonians 5:11 we are told, "Therefore encourage one another and build each other up," but be warned: it is risky to open up in this way. Our self-doubting voice can take over and immobilize us, filling us with fear about how the other person will receive our comments. *What if he thinks I am trying too hard? What if she thinks I am a brownnoser and not genuine? What if he doesn't feel the same way, and I am embarrassed for putting myself out there? What if she misinterprets my comments and thinks I am being patronizing in some way? What if he thinks I am being manipulative and trying to pull for affirmation from him?* When we allow these worries to paralyze us, we withdraw into a self-protective cocoon—one that keeps us detached from other people. When we reach out to others and share specific things we appreciate about them, we are not guaranteed that they will do the same or even feel the same about us. *But we should do it anyway.* When we invite others to be whole people, we can genuinely appreciate their unique gifts, and we honor God when we directly share those things we appreciate with them. We do not tell people what we appreciate about them as a tool to get them to like us. Instead, we share because we want to encourage them to live out their gifts and callings. We want them to know that those gifts are touching others, even if they aren't sure how to receive our affirming comments.

The longing to know others deeply and to be deeply known is the fundamental human desire. It is a reflection of the unique way God has molded us in his image. In the context of relationships we are best able to reflect and image God. At their best, relationships give us a small taste of the love God has for us. Relationships are not just a byproduct of the human journey. They don't just make it easier to get through when we are having a rough time at work or feeling discouraged. Rather, relationships are the *point* of the spiritual journey. One of my psychology professors used to echo, with a slight variation, Bill Clinton's political campaign mantra, "It's the economy, Stupid." "It's the relationship, Stupid," he would say, over and over again. Life is about relationships.

Christ came to earth to form relationships with human people. The Christian life beckons us to engage in a relationship with our Creator. David Benner argues, "Intimate relationships with others prepare us for intimacy with God."[16] Likewise, intimacy with God prepares us for intimacy with other people. We can cultivate intimate relationships by getting to know ourselves and sharing that self in relationships. We can also grow in intimacy by inviting others to be genuine and authentic with us—appreciating, respecting and even celebrating their unique differences and gifts. Although pursuing whole and healthy intimate relationships is hard work and requires us to take risks and be vulnerable, it is worth it. And thankfully, we have a Savior who fills us and empowers us to love with his love. We are called to live life in relationships with others, and we honor God and reflect him well when we heed that call.

TOOLS FOR THE JOURNEY

Take care of yourself. When we don't take care of ourselves, we often unconsciously expect or look for others to take care of us. When we do take care of ourselves, we are better able to reach out to others and allow them to be who they are. By caring for ourselves, we care for others because we free them from having to meet our needs. Parker Palmer writes, "Self-care is never a selfish act—it is simply good stewardship of the only gift I have, the gift I was put on earth to offer to others."[17]

Self-care includes taking care of basic needs, like getting adequate

---

[16]Benner, *Sacred Companions*, p. 41.
[17]Parker Palmer, *Let Your Life Speak: Listening for the Voice of Vocation* (San Francisco: Jossey-Bass, 2000), p. 30.

sleep, eating a balanced diet and exercising. When we don't take care of these needs, we have less energy—less life. Consequently, we have less to give in our relationships. It's amazing how much of a difference this seemingly small, yet so significant, change can make in our ability to be ourselves and allow others to be themselves. Self-care also includes addressing our deeper needs, which are different for everyone. Self-awareness is important because it will help us understand and identify our unique needs. Perhaps you get irritable at the end of the day because you really need some time alone to regroup and decompress. You might find yourself feeling overwhelmed because you have a hard time ever saying no to people. Self-care means knowing when you need a break. Get a babysitter for an afternoon or spend an hour with an old friend to reconnect and catch up.

When we take care of ourselves, we know what we enjoy doing and we find time for it. It means that we make a place in our busy schedules for crossword puzzles, gardening, running or whatever other activity we enjoy doing. For Jenny, an essential way in which she cared for herself was by seeking counseling and taking medication. Only by doing this was she able to effectively reach out to her family and friends in a real way. This does not mean those who loved her didn't support her; it just means that she didn't expect them to fight her fight for her. Look for practical ways to practice self-care, with both your basic needs and your deeper needs.

Value all relationships. One of the ways we can grow toward relational wholeness is by valuing all relationships—not just those with our family and close friends. If we image God best in the context of relationships, then we need to take seriously the importance of every relationship as an opportunity to reflect God's love and grace. We can live out of our whole personhood, and invite others to do the same, in every interpersonal situation. Authenticity is not restricted to relationships with our spouses or children. Rather, we can practice being ourselves, and appreciating and seeing the good in others, in all of our interactions. Manning writes, "In every encounter we either give life or we drain it. There is no neutral exchange. We enhance human dignity, or we diminish it. The success or failure of a given day is measured by the quality of our interest and compassion toward those around us. We define ourselves by our response to human need."[18] Each person we interact with is an image-bearer of God, and we invite that person to be authentic when we treat him or her with respect and dignity.

As you go about your daily activities this week, remind yourself that you can choose to act as a whole person, being genuine, honest and authentic, with each person you meet. You can appreciate and celebrate other people's unique gifts and talents, even those of people you do not know well. Don't restrict your blessings of affirmation to your children or husband. Rather, choose to be an encourager to each person you meet, whether it's the woman who cashes your check at the bank or your oldest friend. If the bank teller is a bit slow with your check or your friend makes a mistake, offer them grace and respect. Every individual you interact with is an amazing creature made in God's image. You grow in wholeness when you treat every relationship with respect and care.

Cultivate a safe space for authentic sharing. Intimacy is found in moments when we feel safe and secure, when we trust enough to share our deepest pains and hurts with another. When the other person is responsive and empathic, we feel heard and understood. These moments of authentic sharing do not simply happen by accident. Rather, we can cultivate intimacy in our relationships by creating a safe space for honest sharing.

Although intimacy is built in moments of authentic sharing, sometimes it is not safe to share the deepest parts of yourself. A professional business environment, for example, is probably not the best place for intimate personal disclosures. If you are meeting a friend at a restaurant or coffee shop, the environment might be so loud or distracting that it would be difficult to stay focused and really listen to each other. You might not want to share deep personal details in an environment that

---

[18]Manning, *Abba's Child*, p. 169.

lacks privacy. In addition to unsafe environments, sometimes people are unsafe. It can be hurtful and damaging to share parts of yourself with a person who does not respect you or your story. When the environment or relationship is not safe, you are right when you choose not to share intimate and painful parts of yourself.

One of the ways you can create a safe space is by communicating that you are genuinely interested in hearing other people's stories. As a therapist, one of the ways I try to communicate my genuine interest in my client's story is by asking questions. When Jenny shared her story with me, I asked a lot of questions so she could clarify or illustrate her story because I wanted to make sure I understood. Other times I asked questions that pushed her to go deeper. I did not ask for details to satisfy my own curiosity. Rather, I asked questions in order to understand her world as she saw it. I wanted Jenny to know that I cared about her and was interested in hearing as much as she wanted to tell me. I did not push Jenny to tell me every detail of her story at once. In fact, it was not until months later that Jenny disclosed that she had been sexually abused as a child. Although I suspected a history of trauma, it was important to me that Jenny chose to share her story when she felt ready. Had I pushed her into sharing before she was ready, this could have traumatized her all over again. I cared for Jenny and wanted to hear her story—when she felt safe enough to share it with me.

By asking meaningful questions of people we care about, we demonstrate that we are interested in their story for them alone, not as an avenue from which to share our own story. We communicate that we care about the hurts they have encountered, not that we are trying to change or fix them by offering pat answers or easy advice. Sometimes it is hard to know what questions to ask to create this kind of safe space. Any question that communicates genuine care and concern can work. Some possibilities might include: "Describe your best childhood memory," "What is the most significant thing God has taught you in the last year?" or "What is an area in which you are growing or changing?" Or you can start with some easier questions about favorite books or movies. Sometimes, however, it is helpful to have suggestions. Bookstores carry a variety of question books that contain hundreds of questions on a broad range of topics. You could even play the Question Game with a group of friends or with your spouse, in which you read a question and everyone at the table answers the question. These kinds of questions invite people to get real. Model openness in your own responses, and affirm and appreciate other people for being honest and authentic with you.

Another way to create a safe space for authentic sharing is by communicating genuine respect and appreciation for others. One way to do this is through an affirmation circle. I have done affirmation circles with my husband, with friends and family members, with clients and small classes. The mechanics are quite simple. Begin with one person, and then have everyone in the circle share something they appreciate, respect or admire about that person. Continue this until each person in the circle has been affirmed by every other member. You can do this in a circle of two or a circle of ten. Be prepared, however, that it might take longer than you think. My husband recently did an affirmation circle at a men's retreat, and he had planned forty-five minutes for it. Instead, he had to move people along to finish it up in a little over two hours! Every time I have done this I have felt more connected and closer to the people in the circle—and not because I get to hear affirmations from others. Although it is encouraging to hear those things about me, the whole experience is about connecting. It is an amazing thing to sit with a group of people who are all speaking blessings of truth to each other.

Whether you are cultivating intimacy by asking questions or affirming others, it is important to ensure that you do this with safe people. You can do many things to cultivate a safe environment, but you can't make other people safe. If you have reason to believe that someone is going to be hurtful, offer affirmations that are really criticisms in disguise, or be unable to participate, then attempting to cultivate intimacy could ultimately be more hurtful than helpful. I would encourage you to begin asking questions, or try an affirmation circle with people who you know reasonably well and who you trust would be able to participate. If you are reading this book with a partner or group, that would be an ideal place to start.

God has created us for intimate connections with others, and we cannot grow in wholeness if we do not grow relationally. By taking care of ourselves, valuing all relationships and creating a safe space for genuine sharing, we can grow healthy intimate relationships. Sometimes, however, our relational difficulties are not due to dissatisfaction or disconnection; rather, our relationships have been a source of overwhelming pain. As much as we may want to cultivate intimacy in our current relationships, the damage from our past paralyzes us. Therefore, I will now turn to the pain of relational wounds and how to begin the restoration process.

10

Restoring Your Broken Heart

HEALING FROM LOSS, ABUSE AND OTHER RELATIONAL WOUNDS

We hear the warnings of our parents, our friends, even our own minds,

but our emotions will rarely be restricted.

We lose ourselves in love.

We love with abandon and, then, love abandons us.

SARA SHANDLER
*OPHELIA SPEAKS: ADOLESCENT GIRLS WRITE
ABOUT THEIR SEARCH FOR SELF*

I remember the night my father left us," Debra, a forty-eight-year-old woman, told me in a quiet voice, several months after she had started seeing me for counseling. "It was right before Christmas and I was nine years old. I had been listening to my parents fight every night—sometimes about me, sometimes about the fact that my father was never around. When my mother told me my father wasn't coming home, it felt like someone had stabbed me in the chest. I remember being so upset that he wasn't going to be there Christmas morning. It's been years since that happened, and now I have a family of my own, but in some ways it feels like that wound never really healed."

Although we were created for relationships, one result of the Fall is that we function in broken ways in relationships. We may have experienced a deep relational loss that has caused us to feel lost as well. We may have been involved in relationships that were hurtful or even abusive. When we are wounded in relationships, through abandonment or death; divorce, breakup or betrayal; or through emotional, physical or sexual abuse, the wounds run deep.

Some of us, like Debra, walk through life with the emotional equivalent of a knife in our chests. We may be unsure how to remove that knife, or we may fear the pain involved in the process. Failing to remove the source of a wound, however, makes us vulnerable to additional pain, such as infection or the spread of disease. If we do not remove the knife in our chest, it can get bumped or pushed with minimal contact, and our wound gets reopened. In *Where Is God When It Hurts?*—Philip Yancey's classic book on suffering—Yancey describes pain as an unusual gift:

> Too often the emotional trauma of intense pain blinds us to its inherent value. When I break an arm and swallow bottles of aspirin to dull the ache, gratitude for pain is not the first thought that comes to mind. Yet at that very moment, pain is alerting my body to the danger, mobilizing anti-infection defenses around the wound, and forcing me to refrain from activities that might further compound the injury. Pain demands the attention that is crucial to my recovery.[1]

Like physical pain, emotional pain awakens our senses. Although numbing efforts can quiet those pains temporarily, they do not provide lasting relief. When we ignore the pain or seek relief through alcohol, food, work, new relationships or a flurry of distracting activities, we are only helped for a time. However, in order to experience genuine healing, we must face our pain directly. In this chapter I will examine ways to heal

---

[1]Philip Yancey, *Where Is God When It Hurts? A Comforting, Healing Guide for Coping with Hard Times* (Grand Rapids: Zondervan, 1990), p. 22.

from relational wounds, such as telling your story, experiencing a broad range of emotions and acknowledging your pain. I will also explore the role of forgiveness in the healing process and the importance of taking risks in future relationships.

TELLING YOUR STORY

If we want to reflect God to the world, we must not fear our wounds but face them. Acknowledging that we have been wounded does not mean we are whining or blaming someone else for our current troubles. Rather, by facing our pain directly, we are taking an active step in beginning the healing process.

When Debra's father left that cold evening so many years ago, all Debra knew was that he was not with them. Not until the next month did Debra discover that her father had actually left for another woman. When her father married that woman a year later, Debra's fantasies that her parents would reconcile and that they would be a family again were crushed. Sitting in the church watching her father marry another woman, Debra felt the knife going in all over again. Debra's father and his new wife decided to start their own family, and they had three children together. Debra used to visit her father on alternate weekends and holidays, but she always felt like just that: a visitor. A few years later, her mother remarried as well. Eventually, her mother and stepfather had two children of their own. Although Debra always felt a special closeness with her mother, she couldn't escape the feeling that she didn't quite belong anywhere.

Debra couldn't wait to grow up so she could start her own family, because she was sure that then she would feel like she belonged. She married her high school sweetheart, Sean, shortly after graduation. Although they stayed together, their marriage has been rocky. Debra has never been able to let go of her fear that Sean is going to leave her, and he has become increasingly frustrated with her inability to trust him. When their children were young, Debra poured herself into them, trying to give them all the love and security she longed for as a child. Sometimes her intensity was overwhelming, and her kids pulled or pushed away as they got older. Debra felt this pulling away as rejection, and it was like that original wound getting bumped and hurting her all over again. Now that all of her children are grown, Debra has realized how much of her identity was wrapped up in her role as a mother. Without children to care for, Debra has felt a bit lost over the last several years. She and Sean are alone in their house, but they have never experienced real intimacy in their relationship. From the outside, Debra knows that it looks like her dreams of security have come true: she has raised three children with her husband of thirty years. But on the inside, Debra feels uncomfortably similar to how she felt as a child—like she doesn't really belong, even in her own home.

If we truly want to find healing from relational wounds, we must first examine those wounds. For Debra to begin removing the knife that was first planted in her chest that night when her father left, she first had to notice the knife and acknowledge its presence. Instead of pretending that her father's abandonment was ancient history and didn't bother her, she had to look directly at the pain and admit how much it had hurt her. Whether we acknowledge our pain or not, those old wounds have a way of resurfacing in our lives.

For Debra, that pain revealed itself in her constant fear that her husband would leave her or her children reject her. Others of us become irritable or depressed without knowing why, or we might feel tense and anxious. Some of us might experience physical symptoms like headaches, sleeping difficulties or back pain. We might find ourselves becoming impatient and critical with our husbands or children. Our service to God and others may feel lifeless and dutiful, rather than joyful and effective.

After noticing the wound and acknowledging its presence, we must then find the courage to, metaphorically speaking, pull the knife out. "It hurt so much when I was a little girl and my father left us," Debra told me as we discussed her healing process. "I'm scared it will hurt just as much to take the knife out as it hurt going in." Debra's fear that removing the knife would be painful was a realistic one. Debra wished that her pain would magically disappear without her involvement, and she had tried this strategy and ignored her wound for forty-one years. Although she feared the pain of trying to remove the knife, leaving it there had caused other kinds of pain in her relationships with her husband and her children. For Debra to find real healing, she had to stop running from her pain. By acknowledging how she had been hurt and allowing herself to feel the pain of those old wounds, Debra realized that God was bigger than her pain. Although she had always believed this intellectually, *feeling* it was an altogether different thing.

It took weeks for Debra to share her whole story with me, and it was a painful process. At times, Debra felt overwhelmed by the sadness, anger and guilt she felt, yet she had the courage to face her painful past and the feelings it brought with it. Lewis Smedes writes, "We need to take responsibility for the pain we feel: Decide what we are going to do with it—hold on to it, get even for it, or heal it. When we have owned our pain, we are ready to do something else with it."[2] Debra was ready to do something with her pain and was tired of it quietly controlling her. By facing that pain directly, Debra discovered that she could confront her pain and not be destroyed in the process. Debra was stronger than she had believed herself to be, and this discovery was healing in and of itself.

Although facing our wounds is essential, we do not need to—nor should we—do it alone. By acknowledging our pain to others and allowing them to walk alongside us, we allow God to use his hands and feet to speak comfort and strength to our fear and sadness. Admitting our need and asking for help can be frightening, but by doing so, we allow God to minister to us in powerful ways. In her memoir, Anne Lamott describes how God used a Christian man to help her at a time in her life when she was suicidal and an alcoholic. While talking with that man years later, he recalled his impression of her: "You said your prayers weren't working anymore, and I could see that in your desperation you

---

[2]Lewis Smedes, *The Art of Forgiving: When You Need to Forgive and Don't Know How* (New York: Ballantine Books, 1996), pp. 135-36.

were trying to save *yourself:* so I said you should stop praying for a while, and let me pray for you. And right away, you seemed to settle down inside."[3] By acknowledging her pain and asking for help, Lamott allowed this man to support her in a way she could not support herself.

Some of us, however, may fear allowing others to be part of our healing journey. We may have tried to share our pain with someone in the past but were hurt in the process. When Debra was a young adult, she confided in a friend about the pain of her parents' divorce, and the friend told Debra to lighten up and get over it: "Lots of people's parents get divorced, Deb. Stop making such a big deal about it and move on. They obviously have!" Although her friend may have had good intentions, those words wounded Debra all over again. In some ways, those words drove the knife back into Debra's heart, just as it was beginning to work its way out. Debra's hurt was real, but she learned from this interaction that sharing her hurt wasn't safe.

Sometimes, though, we can also get locked in past pain because of *how* we tell our stories. A trusted friend or counselor can help us reframe the telling in ways that are not just cathartic, but allow us to move toward healing and growth—especially if it regrounds our pain in the story of our creation and renewal in the image of Christ. For example, when Debra initially came to see me for counseling, she told me that she was having some "empty nest" adjustment issues and wanted help developing a better relationship with her husband. It took Debra time before she trusted me enough to share the source of her pain. Even when she told me about her parents' divorce, Debra expected me to think she was overreacting and thus minimized its importance: "I know this isn't a big deal," she said as she began her story. Yet as Debra shared her hurt, I knew it *was* a big deal. Underneath Debra's self-protective defensiveness was a nine-year-old girl whose world was falling apart. Over the course of our relationship, Debra and I talked about how painful and lonely

---

[3]Anne Lamott, *Traveling Mercies: Some Thoughts on Faith* (New York: Pantheon Books, 1999), p. 43.

those early years were for her. We discussed the impact her parents' divorce and remarriages had on her relationship with her own husband and children. Because Debra took a risk and acknowledged her pain to me, she learned that it could be safe to open up to others. After allowing me to walk alongside her and share in her pain, Debra eventually began sharing more of herself with her husband and allowing him to be part of her healing process as well.

When we have been wounded in relationships, through loss, rejection or abuse, the first step toward healing is acknowledging the wound. Although it can be frightening and painful, true healing requires that we examine the wound. Rather than trying to ignore, numb or suppress the pain, we must allow ourselves to feel those painful emotions. Finally, true healing requires that we allow others to share our pain and walk with us through it. A counselor may be the best person for you to talk through your pain with for the first time. It is especially important to talk with a professional counselor if you are reliving the trauma through nightmares or flashbacks or chronically numbing your pain through alcohol or drugs. If you are having thoughts of hurting yourself or having difficulty functioning because of your depressed or anxious feelings, then professional counseling and possibly medication would be the best course of action. It is wise to choose carefully who you will share your pain with, but choose *someone,* and allow him or her to journey with you toward healing.

CLEANING OUT THE WOUNDS

After acknowledging the presence of the wounds our relational hurts have left behind, allowing ourselves to experience a broad range of emotions, and inviting a trusted confidante to walk with us and share our pain, we can then begin to clean out the wound. Although cleaning a physical wound is often painful, it allows us to see if the wound has spread or become infected. I grew up with three older brothers, and they tended to be a bit more adventuresome than I. One afternoon, I got in a minor biking accident. When my brothers fell off their bikes, they just kept playing, and in fact, sometimes it seemed that they fell off their bikes on purpose! However, I was a bit softer. With tears streaming down my face, I ran home to tell my mother what had happened to me, and what do you think she did when she saw my bloody knees and tear-stained cheeks? She cleaned my wounds. This was not my first choice, because cleaning hurts! But she did it anyway because she wanted to protect me from further injury and ensure proper healing. She comforted me as she poured peroxide over my scrapes. Even though it stung, she wanted to get rid of the bad stuff—the bacteria and germs—that could keep my wounds from healing. Relational wounds can also get infected and need cleaning. Genuine healing comes in part from letting go of the bad stuff—the bacteria and germs—our relational wounds have left behind.

Relationship wounds and negative relational patterns. Sometimes the bad stuff we need to let go of is the relationship itself. Perhaps you had an abusive parent or an unfaithful husband, and you needed to leave the relationship in order to begin the journey toward healing. Or perhaps the bad stuff is not the relationship itself, but relationship *patterns*. Debra's relationship patterns were rooted in her unmet longing for security in childhood. Debra's relational insecurity did not end when she became an adult. Rather, she constantly struggled with fears of abandonment and rejection in her relationships—even when that fear was unjustified. Sometimes her fears became so intense that loved ones pulled away from her, thus confirming and intensifying her original fears. For Debra to experience real healing from her past relational hurts, she had to acknowledge her own relationship pattern of unrealistic fear and insecurity. By taking responsibility for her part in maintaining some of her hurts in current relationships, Debra was empowered. If Debra was merely a victim of other people's bad decisions and hurtful actions, she would have no hope that things could get better. By identifying maladaptive relational patterns that she tended to fall into, however, Debra was able to see ways that she could effect change in her own life. As Debra became more aware of her pattern of pulling away emotionally from her husband out of her fear that he was going to leave her, she began to make conscious choices to *not* withdraw from him. When she felt her anxiety and insecurity building, she reminded herself of her husband's faithfulness and commitment to her. Debra began to intentionally share her honest feelings and thoughts with her husband, even when it made her feel scared and unsure. Her husband, in turn, started sharing more of himself with her, and they began to experience a greater intimacy than they had known before.

Although our experiences and wounds may be quite different from Debra's, we all engage in relationship patterns based on our internal working models of who we are, and who we expect others to be, in relationships. Relationship patterns themselves are not bad. However, when those patterns are overly rigid and become wounding to us or to others, identifying them and letting them go can aid us in the healing process.

Perhaps your childhood home was filled with conflict, and you learned to be the master peacemaker. When people are upset, you know how to calm them down and ease the tension. Whether you are with family or friends, church members or coworkers, you do what needs to be done to keep everyone happy. Sometimes this means ignoring your own needs or opinions; sometimes it means being misleading or telling white lies. Often it leads to superficial relationships in which people do not know the real you.

Or perhaps you tend to be a people-helper. If people are hurting or lost, you are the one who seeks them out. Yet instead of developing long-lasting meaningful relationships, you go from one person to the next—helping others but never allowing them to really know you in the process.

Or maybe you grew up with an insulting and verbally abusive father, and you now find yourself in a series of romantic relationships with men who treat you badly. As much as you want to find a kind man, it seems that you keep playing out the same drama with new men.

In order to heal from the relational wounds of the past, we need to identify and let go of the relational patterns we fall into that reopen old wounds in current relationships. A safe and trusting relationship is the best place to explore those maladaptive relational patterns. Whether you do this with a counselor or trusted friend, you need someone who will be honest with you, someone who can help you get outside yourself to examine objectively the harmful patterns that are replaying themselves in your life. That kind of honest relationship is not always an easy one, but it will be a growing one. When my accountability partner, Brittney, notices a particular pattern of relating in my life that is keeping me from healthy and whole relationships, she cares about me enough to tell me what she sees. Together we talk about where those patterns might have developed and how to begin taking steps to break them. Relationships are the context in which we grow and change, and in my relationship with Brittney, I am able to take the first steps toward identifying and changing negative relational patterns. You, too, can make changes. And having a supportive and trusted person in your corner to talk and pray with is essential.

Forgiveness. In addition to unhealthy relationships and relationship patterns, another harmful element that can lead to infection and disease is the bitterness and resentment—even hate—that our relational wounds have left behind. In order to experience genuine healing and freedom from our painful past, we have to find a way to let go of those insidious emotions. When we are wounded in horrible and unfair ways by unremorseful offenders, the idea of forgiveness may seem like a dirty joke. Yet the reality is that the choice *not* to forgive usually damages us more than anyone else. As Lewis Smedes writes, "When we forgive, we set a prisoner free and discover that the prisoner we set free is us."[4]

Choosing to forgive does not mean that we forget what happened to us. It does not mean that we excuse the people who hurt us and say that their actions were okay. Forgiveness is not the same as reconciliation, and it does not mean that we pretend the hurts never happened. Forgiveness does not mean we ignore our wounds or allow others to hurt

---

[4]Smedes, *Art of Forgiving*, p. 178.

us repeatedly. What, then, does forgiveness mean? Much research and writing has actually been done on this topic, and after reviewing the literature on forgiveness, a team of researchers argue that forgiveness is built on one core feature: "When people forgive, their responses toward (or, in other words, what they think of, feel about, want to do to, or actually do to) people who have offended or injured them become more positive and less negative."[5]

Forgiveness begins with God. When we forgive, we hand ourselves over to God, trusting that God alone can restore and heal us fully and completely. Ultimately, the sins committed against us are powerless to prevent us from having lives that fully glorify God. When we forgive, we are also trusting that God is totally and completely opposed to evil and sees it whenever and wherever it occurs. We agree with God that what happened to us ought not to have happened. When we forgive, we are not asking God to let anyone or anything off the hook. Yet we also recognize that God separates human beings from their evil acts, so all of us (including those who have hurt us) are able to be delivered from the power of sin. Therefore, when we forgive we also hand the offending person over to God.

Forgiveness allows us to look at ourselves honestly: as broken children of God who are first and foremost forgiven creatures. Empowered by Christ's work and his love for us, forgiveness allows us to replace our negative responses with more positive ones. As pastoral counselor John Patton points out:

> The believer is surprisingly empowered to be forgiving. Human forgiveness, understood in this theological way, is not primarily something to be done to improve our health or secure our salvation, but it is an illustration of a quality of life when it is lived in relation to God and one's fellow human beings. . . . Human forgive-

---

[5]Michael McCullough, Kenneth Pargament and Carl Thoresen, "The Psychology of Forgiveness: History, Conceptual Issues, and Overview" in *Forgiveness: Theory, Research, and Practice*, ed. Michael McCullough, Kenneth Pargament and Carl Thoresen (New York: Guilford Press, 2000), p. 9.

ness is not a condition of God's forgiveness but something enabled by God's response to human life.[6]

As the Lord's Prayer says, "Forgive us our debts, / as we also have forgiven our debtors" (Matthew 6:12). We are forgiven people. When we forgive, we reflect God's grace and mercy to the world around us. By choosing to forgive, we give God our hurts and allow him to walk with us. Forgiveness allows us to let go of the burdens of bitterness and resentment and lay them at the feet of Jesus, one who understands and even bears our suffering and pain.

Sometimes the person we blame most for our pain is ourselves. When the person who was hurtful or abusive to us is someone we valued and loved, we may not have felt safe being angry at them. Instead, we may have turned that anger inward and blamed ourselves. *If only I had been a better-behaved child, my parents would not have gotten divorced. If I could have been more sexually fulfilling, he would not have had that affair. I loved the special attention he gave me, and it's my own fault that it happened; I can't really call that abuse.* Healing from relational pain requires us to look at ourselves honestly. Forgiveness means letting go of the unfair anger, blame and resentment we might have placed on ourselves. Forgiveness is essential to the healing process, but we cannot heal unless we know who hurt us. As Everett Worthington writes, forgiveness requires you to "admit that a wrong was done to you."[7] By constantly blaming ourselves for wounds that were inflicted by others, we keep ourselves from finding real freedom. Sometimes in the process of trying to manage our own pain and protect ourselves from future pain, we end up wounding others. Forgiving ourselves for our relational wounds does not mean that we excuse ourselves for intentional hurt we caused another person through our words and actions. When we hurt others, we need to repent and

---

[6]John Patton, "Forgiveness in Pastoral Care and Counseling," in *Forgiveness: Theory, Research, and Practice,* ed. Michael McCullough, Kenneth Pargament and Carl Thoresen (New York: Guilford Press, 2000), p. 290.

[7]Everett Worthington, *Forgiving and Reconciling: Bridges to Wholeness and Hope* (Downers Grove, Ill.: InterVarsity Press, 2003), p. 73.

seek forgiveness from them, but we also need to be aware of when we are blaming ourselves unjustly.

Not only do we blame ourselves for old wounds and hurts, but many of us also feel resentful and angry toward God. We may know theologically that God loves us perfectly, but when faced with unthinkable pain it can feel like God has left us. When we feel hopeless and lost in pain, we can harbor bitter feelings toward God. Smedes suggests that our angry feelings toward God can come in many forms:

> We do hate God sometimes. All of us, I think. On the sly. If we dare not hate the Giver, we do dare hate his gifts. We hate his world. Or we hate ourselves. When we shut our eyes to every reason we have for being glad to be alive, when we resent good things that happen to our friends, when our hearts stifle every happy impulse, we are nurturing a passive hatred of God.[8]

When we are unable to experience joy in God's good gifts, we are living in unforgiveness. When we harbor anger toward God and his gifts, we may also feel guilty, which only intensifies our sense of the distance between God and us. So at a time when we are hurting and broken, most in need of God's comfort and guidance, we may be unable to even see the hand he holds out to us.

Healing from our wounds, therefore, requires that we honestly face our feelings toward God—even if we are uncomfortable with those hurt or angry feelings. I believe that God loves me perfectly and completely and does not deserve blame for the bad things that happen in our world; I also believe that God is sovereign. It is difficult to reconcile those two things sometimes. Now this is not a theology text, and I am neither qualified nor able to provide a comprehensive philosophical answer to the problem of pain, but this is what I do know: God is big enough to handle all my questions and doubts, my fears and anger. Only by laying those

---

[8]Lewis Smedes, *Forgive & Forget: Healing the Hurts We Don't Deserve* (New York: Pocket Books, 1990), p. 114.

at his feet am I able to trust him and find freedom from those things. God doesn't need our forgiveness, but sometimes *we* need to let go of our anger and resentment toward God. "When you forgive God," Smedes writes, "you just live in the silence, and grope toward the goodness of life, and believe that, in spite of everything, he is your friend."[9]

True healing requires that we not only let go of the bad stuff from hurtful relationships but that we hold on to the good stuff. When someone has been hurtful or abusive to us, it may seem unthinkable that there is any good stuff to hold on to. Yet in every hurtful situation we learn lessons about ourselves. In our brokenness, there is purpose—and this purpose can give meaning to our pain, even as we heal and move away from that pain. From her parents' divorce and remarriage, Debra learned to value relationships. She was not a perfect mother, but she cherished her children and protected her family. When I work with people in counseling, one of the most important things I do is try to help people find hope. And one of the most important sources of hope is discovering something beautiful in the midst of our pain and hurt. Those lessons are different for each of us. From loss we can learn that life is a precious gift. From living through abuse we can learn that we are survivors.

Now I've heard some people turn these lessons into a *reason* for the pain, which is a very different thing, which I will discuss more fully in chapter eleven. A young woman I saw in counseling after her father was killed was horrified by some of the comments church members made after his death. "Your father is in a better place, and perhaps God allowed your father to die to bring you closer to God," one of the elders told her. Learning good things through pain does not mean that God brought that pain *in order* to teach those lessons. We can learn through the painful experiences in our lives, and this is one of the good things we can hold on to. This does not mean, however, that God allowed that pain *so that* we would learn a few life lessons.

Healing requires not only that we hold on to the good stuff but that

[9]Ibid., p. 123.

we draw on our hope and courage to choose to love again. When we love, we are vulnerable. Others may hurt or betray us, leave us or die. Our hearts may be broken. Love disappoints us. Yet the truth is that we are made for relationships, and life is not worth living without them. The key to genuine healing from past relational wounds is to find the courage to really love again. Take risks, make mistakes and be vulnerable—with other people, with yourself and with God.

TOOLS FOR THE JOURNEY

Write your autobiography. Pain is overwhelming, and confronting that pain directly and honestly can be frightening. Therefore, when we have been deeply hurt in a relationship, sometimes we do whatever we need to in order to avoid additional pain. We may drown our pain in activities or substances or gossip. We may try to suppress our pain and act as if it never happened. Yet in order to truly move on and get past our pain, we must take a hard and honest look back at that pain. When we have been wounded and we keep silent, those wounds only gain more power over us. Things that are kept in the dark have the power to ignite terror and shame in us. Only by bringing them into the light can we truly heal from them.

One practical way to bring those wounds into the light and tell your story is by writing an autobiography. Start at the beginning and write everything you remember about your childhood. If it seems important, write it down. Do not judge yourself or your memories. Do not edit or proofread your story. Just write. Let the memories and the feelings come. Welcome them and invite them because they will make your story more real, more authentic. Even though it will be painful to reexperience the wounds in your own story, it will also help remind you where you have come from and how you have grown through it. Pain can cause us to lose sight of the big picture sometimes because pain is so immediate. By stepping back and outside of your hurts, you can get a greater sense of the big picture of your life.

After you have completely finished writing your story, take time to go back over it. Sometimes therapists talk about how, when we review our life stories, we really see two different stories being woven together. Our good story is made up of the positive things that have happened to us and the things we have done that have allowed us to enjoy life and relationships. Our bad story is made up of the hurtful things that have happened to us and the things we have done that have kept us from enjoying life and relationships.

Sharing your story with someone is also a great way to allow another person to walk with you in your pain. It can also help to hear someone else's perspective. You may want to ask yourself some of the following questions:

- What can I learn from my story?
- When I reflect on my life, do I tend to focus primarily on my bad story? (There is a good story there, so if you are missing it, go back and focus on your good story.)
- Are there patterns in my relationships that I had not noticed before?

Sometimes we are so close to our hurts that we might have a harder time finding, for example, our good story. Your trusted confidante might be able to help you identify pieces of your good story. The following questions are aspects that can be part of your good story:

- In what ways did I grow or become stronger through my experiences?
- Are there people who surprised me along the way?
- Where is God in my story?

After reviewing your story, think about what you would like the next chapters to look like—where would you like to go from here? Spend some time writing out your hopes for future chapters. Do not censor yourself, but let yourself dream and hope, and allow God to quietly move you. His vision of us is so often bigger than ours. So let him move in you as you consider where to go from here. How can you continue the healing process and really choose to live and love again? As you go about your day, be mindful of the fact that you are an unfinished book, and you have the power to make choices to move toward a story of hope and healing. This does not mean that you can control the future. It does not guarantee that only good things will happen to you. But it does remind you that you have power to choose how you will respond to the world around you. With God's help, you can make choices about the kind of story you are writing.

REACH for forgiveness. As you review your own story, one particular issue you might want to attend to is any bitterness or resentment you struggle with. Do you find yourself harboring bitter feelings toward another person, God or yourself? One of the reasons we sometimes hold on to our bitterness and anger is that we have never allowed ourselves to express it. Of course, just saying the words will not make the hurt go away. But hiding from or ignoring the hurt is sure to keep it close at hand.

Another reason some of us have difficulty letting go of the bad stuff from relational wounds is that we begin to feel like we *are* our wounds. Even though it sounds strange, to let go of those wounds can be frightening because they are familiar and comfortable. However, you are more than your hurts. By stepping back to tell your story, you can get perspective and a little distance from those wounds.

After telling your story, you probably found some things you need to let go of from your old wounds. As much as we mess up and need to be forgiven by God and others, we also need to forgive others. But forgiveness is hard! Lewis Smedes, in his classic text on forgiveness, says that when we forgive we do it slowly and it doesn't happen all at once. Sometimes we're still angry after we forgive, and forgiveness certainly can't be forced, or else it's not real forgiveness. Smedes suggests that when we do forgive, we come as close as possible to God's power of creation:

> For we create a new beginning of our past pain that never had a right to exist in the first place. We create healing for the future by changing a past that had no possibility in it for anything but sick-

ness and death. When we forgive we ride the crest of love's cosmic wave; we walk in stride with God. And we heal the hurt we never deserved.[10]

Although forgiveness is hard, it is worth it. By releasing our bitterness and hate, we are able to move forward in love and hope.

One way you can begin working toward forgiveness is by writing a letter to whomever your anger and blame is targeted at. It may be that you need to write more than one letter. You might need to write to another person, to God or to yourself. Use your letter to tell the recipient how you were hurt. Tell him or her what you needed but did not receive. Use that letter to release your bitterness and anger. Smedes suggests that when we forgive, we let go of our longing for vengeance—our desire to get even for the wrongs committed against us.[11] Vengeance is never satisfying because, even if we hurt the offending parties, it never feels equal to the original hurt they caused us. Therefore, another important use of your letter is to try and let go of your longing to get even. When I ask women I counsel to write a letter to someone who has hurt them, they do not often actually send the letter. Instead, they use the exercise as an opportunity to give voice to their hurts, to examine them and the impact they have had on their current relationships. They use the letter to begin the forgiveness process. They understand that this exercise is not a miracle cure. It will not change what happened to them, but it is a start. And we all need somewhere to start.

Everett Worthington offers another great place to start the forgiveness process. Worthington is a psychologist who has written extensively on forgiveness, but he has also grappled with the struggle to forgive in his own life. In his book *Forgiving and Reconciling,* Worthington tells the story of his own forgiveness process after his mother was brutally murdered.[12] Worthington presents a pyramid model to "REACH" forgiveness

---

[10]Smedes, *Forgive & Forget*, pp. 191-92; for further reading on how we forgive, see also pp. 125-58.

[11]Smedes, *Art of Forgiving*, pp. 7-10.

[12]Worthington, *Forgiving and Reconciling*.

based on his years of clinical and research experience, as well as on his own personal experience with forgiveness. REACH is an acronym for the components of forgiveness, and it is a helpful tool for thinking through the forgiveness process in your own life.[13]

- *Recall the hurt.* Worthington discusses the importance of naming your hurts instead of denying them or minimizing them.
- *Empathize.* Worthington suggests that, in order to experience true forgiveness, it helps to try and understand the humanness of the person who hurt you.
- *Offer the Altruistic gift of forgiveness.* Remember that you are a forgiven person. After reflecting on what it feels like when *you* are forgiven by a friend or loved one for an offense, consider giving the gift of forgiveness to someone else.
- *Commit publicly to forgive.* Worthington argues that you are less likely to doubt your forgiveness if you make your commitment to forgive public. Tell another person, tell God and tell yourself that you have forgiven. You can also symbolize your forgiveness through, for example, a certificate of forgiveness, a letter or a poem.
- *Hold on to forgiveness.* Even when you feel like your forgiveness is slipping, remind yourself of your commitment. Remembering hurts is not the same as unforgiveness.

Forgiveness is not a quick and easy process. There is no formula or technique that will allow you to quickly forgive someone and move on with your life. You cannot forgive unless you are ready and willing to do it. However, when you have become tired of carrying your bitterness and resentment around with you and are ready to lay it down, you can hold the hand of Jesus and practice laying your burdens at his feet.

Hope. Hope. Hope. If there is a singular answer to the hurts and wounds in our lives, that answer is hope. Hope is the essence of Chris-

---

[13]See Worthington, *Forgiving and Reconciling,* for a comprehensive examination of his REACH model.

tianity: "To them God has chosen to make known among the Gentiles the glorious riches of this mystery, which is Christ in you, the hope of glory" (Colossians 1:27). One of the worst things about pain and hurt is that it leaves us hopeless. We fear that we will never be loved in the way we long to feel loved—the way God has created us to be loved. We fear we will never able to love someone else the way we were made to love. We worry that the pain will never go away, and we will always hurt the way we do now. We feel utterly alone, like there is no one who fully understands our pain. To find hope is to open our eyes and look for a reason to live. Even when those reasons seem slim and are hard to find, we look for them! We look for the kind of hope Job spoke of after facing innumerable sufferings and calling out to God in the midst of them, "Though he slay me, yet will I hope in him" (Job 13:15). Hope that things can get better. Hope that we will be loved. Hope that we will be able to love again. Hope that we can be happy. Hope that we can trust others and not be punished for doing so.

Even when we feel scared and hopeless, if we want to find healing, then we need hope. Find hope where you can. Hope in your *desire* for health and wholeness, because God has planted that longing for wholeness in you. Hope in the promises God offers, " 'For I know the plans I have for you,' declares the LORD, 'plans to prosper you and not to harm you, plans to give you hope and a future' " (Jeremiah 29:11). Look for hope and cling to it wherever you see a glimpse of it. When there is something good in your life, however small, celebrate that good thing. Did you get out of bed and long for a warm cup of coffee this morning? Be grateful for that desire, because it is a window to the hope your soul is capable of. Did you feel cared for when your husband brought dinner home for you? Even though your relationship is not perfect, look for the good things that you have together.

Relationships can cause us unmanageable pain, but they can also bring a joy unlike any we have ever known. When we have been hurt in unfair ways, a healthy intimate relationship can provide a soothing balm to our wounded heart. Hope that God will bring safe people into your life. Hope for more peace, more love and more hope. Pray that God will fill you with hope, even when you feel most hopeless, and then look for him acting in your world.

11

Wholly Broken . . . Yet Still Whole

REACHING OUT TO A HURTING WORLD

What I need more than a reasonable explanation of why we feel so much pain

is simple courage to put out my hand and walk hand in hand

through the suffering with my divine Fellow Sufferer. . . .

I have come to believe that the only workable response to unfair pain is hope.

Hope for what? Hope for the time when pointless and unfair suffering

no longer happens. In the crunch, when we see no clear evidence

that this is where he is leading us, hope becomes a kind of courage.

Courage to trust God with our hopes.

LEWIS SMEDES
THE ART OF FORGIVING:
WHEN YOU NEED TO FORGIVE AND DON'T KNOW HOW

When I was seventeen years old, I fell in love for the first time. I met John Wilhelm on a summer conference with my youth group, and I fell hard for him. John overwhelmed me with his life and energy. "I'm going to be president some day," he told me on one of our first walks together. Charismatic and incredibly smart, I believed him. John was passionate about his relationships with God, his family and his friends. He was honest and genuine, and he valued authenticity above all else in relationships. "You're so real," was John's highest compliment. He was good-looking and funny, and I was completely swept off my feet. John was also getting ready to start his freshman year at the University of Michigan, which I thought made him even more sophisticated and exciting. When John pursued me, I could not believe how lucky I was to be with him. John was everything I had dreamed of in a boyfriend, and it was only a matter of weeks before I was convinced that he was my future husband.

Although we lived an hour apart, John drove to see me frequently. He took me to homecoming and prom, and I visited him in Ann Arbor and cheered with him at Michigan football games. John brought me flowers, took me on romantic dates and threw me a surprise eighteenth birthday party. Even better, John possessed a spiritual maturity I had not seen in other guys my age. We went to Bible studies and prayed together. I thought he was the perfect boyfriend, and when I was accepted at Michigan, I could not wait to get to Ann Arbor so we could see each other all the time. However, a few months before I started college, John broke up with me. My fantasies of our life together were shot down, and I was devastated. I had no idea what it felt like, until John, to really have your heart broken. "You'll get over it," said well-meaning friends. "You'll meet someone better. It's good to find out now. There are lots of fish in the sea. Time will heal. You don't want to be tied down when you're at college anyway." These words were offered in love by people who cared for me. However, the words seemed empty as I cried myself to sleep at night, grieving the loss of my first love and what now appeared to be naïve hopes.

A few months later when I moved to Ann Arbor, I avoided John because it hurt even to see him. But, just like those friends had said, it did get better. Slowly and gradually, I noticed that it did not hurt quite so much. I eventually stopped avoiding John, and over the course of the year, we started to become friends again. The next summer, however, John's life was dramatically altered. While on a missions trip with Campus Crusade for Christ, John was hiking in the mountains with some friends. And he fell. He fell 150 feet. The fall left his body untouched in some ways—he did not break a bone. But it ripped his life apart in other ways. John was in a coma for months; he suffered severe brain damage. He was unable to speak or even to swallow.

When John broke up with me the summer before I started college, it was awful. My heart broke in a million different ways. But when John got in that accident, it changed me. John's story is not about me in any significant way, and my experience is nothing compared to those who love him best. However, John's accident was one of the first times I dealt with—and have continued to deal with—the reality of overwhelming pain and brokenness in my own life.

The brokenness that comes when people's lives are ravaged by pain is not something I hear addressed often in church sermons or chapel addresses. It is not a feel-good topic, but as a therapist, it is absolutely unavoidable. One of the privileges, and burdens, of being a counselor is that people invite me into their lives, often during seasons of brokenness. I think of the seemingly countless women who have shared their stories of sexual abuse—abuse by fathers, family friends, grandfathers or even pastors. I think of those who have come to me after their lives were ripped apart by infidelity. I think of the men and women who have lost children or spouses or other loved ones unexpectedly and cannot seem to recover. I also think of those whose lives have been destroyed by mental illness or addiction to alcohol or drugs or sex—their own or a spouse's or child's. And then I also think of those I have sat with whose stories were smaller, who did not necessarily have big "events" happen to them, and yet they were lost and in pain without knowing why. Of course, you do not have to be a therapist to know something about pain. Undoubtedly, some of you reading this now are very acquainted with pain. We are fallen people who live in a fallen world. As a result, things are not the way they are supposed to be and we face pain of all kinds.

With the reality of the brokenness I have experienced in my own life, that which I have been invited into as a counselor, and with an awareness that no person reading this book has been untouched by pain, I would like to close our study of wholeness by taking an honest look at brokenness. It can be tempting to think of brokenness as the opposite of wholeness. If you are like me, you may harbor the secret and futile hope that the path toward wholeness bypasses pain. Your goal in reading this book may have been to get things together precisely so you could avoid pain. My hope is that you have learned some things about avoiding *unnecessary* pain and growing in your relationships, thoughts, sexuality and self-confidence.

The journey toward wholeness, however, is not a pain-free one. When we examine the perfect image of God in Christ, we find our only example of a truly whole and holy life. And Christ's life was characterized by suffering and pain. As believers, we join with Christ by sharing in his sufferings (Romans 8:17). Brokenness, therefore, is not something we can escape or avoid; rather, it is an essential part of the Christian journey. The psalmist writes, "My sacrifice, O God, is a broken spirit; / a broken and contrite heart" (Psalm 51:17). Part of becoming whole is accepting and even incorporating the broken parts of us and using them to inform our service. I am not going to solve the problem of pain in the next few pages, but I would like to honestly explore brokenness: the effect it can have on us, what God can do through it and how we as Christians can most effectively respond to pain and brokenness in the world around us.

BROKENNESS MAKES US HONEST

Philip Yancey calls pain "the gift nobody wants," and one of the gifts of pain is that it makes us honest about our need.[1] Most of us do not ask for times of pain and brokenness. Yet when I reflect on seasons of growth in my own life, I often find that the fertilizer for that growth is pain. When I am broken, I am desperate. Feeling lost and without hope, I open myself up to God in a more radical way than when things are going

---

[1]Philip Yancey, *Where Is God When It Hurts? A Healing, Comforting Guide for Coping with Hard Times* (Grand Rapids: Zondervan, 1990), p. 11.

well in my life. Brokenness reminds me that I cannot make it on my own. I wish I did not need pain to remind me of this. I wish that I walked through each day with a constant awareness of my utter dependency on God for every breath. But I do not. Instead, I breeze through my life, feeling pride in my accomplishments and my relationships. Cornelius Plantinga calls this functional godlessness: "When we are in that stage, God does not seem very real to us. So we do not pray. The less we pray, the less real God seems to us, the duller our sense of responsibility becomes, and thus the duller our sense of ignoring God becomes. It's important to emphasize that the loss is ours."[2] Too often it is only in the face of failure or loss that I am reminded of my complete and utter need for God. Brokenness forces me to give up the fantasy that I am in control, and it makes me acknowledge the truth of God's sovereignty and place my faith in his goodness—even when my life seems like it is falling apart.

When I have been lost in pain, one woman in Scripture has touched me over and over again with her honesty and boldness. Three of the Gospels tell her story, and in it we see a broken woman with a deep awareness of her need for something beyond herself:

> A large crowd followed and pressed around him. And a woman was there who had been subject to bleeding for twelve years. She had suffered a great deal under the care of many doctors and had spent all she had, yet instead of getting better she grew worse. When she heard about Jesus, she came up behind him in the crowd and touched his cloak, because she thought, "If I just touch his clothes, I will be healed." Immediately her bleeding stopped and she felt in her body that she was freed from her suffering.
>
> At once Jesus realized that power had gone out from him. He turned around in the crowd and asked, "Who touched my clothes?"
>
> "You see the people crowding against you," his disciples answered, "and yet you can ask, 'Who touched me?'"

---

[2]Cornelius Plantinga Jr., *Not the Way It's Supposed to Be: A Breviary of Sin* (Grand Rapids: Eerdmans, 1995), p. 195.

But Jesus kept looking around to see who had done it. Then the
woman, knowing what had happened to her, came and fell at his
feet and, trembling with fear, told him the whole truth. He said to
her, "Daughter, your faith has healed you. Go in peace and be freed
from your suffering." (Mark 5:24-34)

This is a woman who had been struggling with the pain of constant
bleeding for twelve years. As bad as these physical symptoms would be
for anyone, she was also part of a culture where bleeding was considered
unclean. According to the mandates of Leviticus 15, any man that even
touched this woman should have immediately returned home and
cleansed himself. Although we know she was hurting, there is a lot we
do not know about this woman. We do not know, for example, if she was
married. What we do know is that she would have been banned from
physical intimacy with her husband for all those years of bleeding. We
also do not know her age or if she already had children. However, assuming her bleeding was of a feminine nature, we can imagine she was
also suffering from infertility during these twelve years. In a culture
where women had few rights and gained respect primarily through bear-
ing children, this was a particularly painful burden. This woman had
been going to doctor after doctor, searching for answers and for help, yet
she had found nothing. Even worse, she had run out of money, and her
symptoms were worsening.

When all her circumstances should have made her hopeless, this
woman's actions demonstrated a radical hope and trust. We sense her
desperation, not just because of the reality of her circumstances but because of what she did. She touched a man, and not just any man, but a
rabbi and spiritual leader. She knew she was breaking religious law by
touching a man, which is presumably why she did not initially come forward when Jesus asked who touched him. Breaking the religious law is
why she fell at his feet "trembling with fear." In her brokenness, however,
this woman became deeply aware of her need for help, and it allowed
her to act in a radically courageous way.

Like the hemorrhaging woman, overwhelming pain makes me desperately aware of my need for help. In his famous work on suffering, *The Problem of Pain,* C. S. Lewis suggests that God uses pain to get our attention: "God whispers to us in our pleasures, speaks in our conscience, but shouts in our pain; it is His megaphone to rouse a deaf world."[3] Pain does rouse us, doesn't it? The pain of John's accident certainly roused me. Although I was a Christian, my relationship with God had taken a distant backseat to the excitement of college life. But John's accident woke me up. I had never spent so much time studying Scripture as I did after John's accident—and not to get closer to God or to worship. Rather, I was looking for an answer. I wanted to know why.

I began asking questions I had been too afraid to ask before. I asked just about anyone who would listen—my parents, my friends, my campus ministry leaders, my pastor. Not everyone was receptive to my questioning. Renee Altson, a woman who grew up with the unspeakable pain of a father who raped her while saying the Lord's Prayer, describes in her vivid memoir *stumbling toward faith* how her questions made people in the church uncomfortable:

> they didn't want to confront their own questions, their own doubts, and they labeled me dangerous. i was considered a troublemaker. . . . slowly i began to see that their problem wasn't with me or with my questions as much as it was with the inevitable (but never verbalized) answer: "i don't know."[4]

As I struggled to make sense of John's accident, I heard a lot of frustrating platitudes about God working in mysterious ways and his ways being higher than our ways. I understood and even believed the scriptural basis of these words, but they still did not offer any real answer. To be perfectly honest, these answers often angered me. They seemed trite and condescending in the face of John's accident. I wanted to ask if they

---

[3]C. S. Lewis, *The Problem of Pain* (New York: Macmillan, 1962), p. 93.
[4]Renee Altson, *Stumbling Toward Faith: My Longing to Heal from the Evil That God Allowed* (Grand Rapids: Zondervan, 2004), p. 59.

would look John's father in the face and say, "God is working in mysterious ways in your son" as John lay unconscious beside him. The sad reality is that many well-meaning Christian people would, and did, say
such things to John's family.

In my own journey, however, I was also blessed with people who re-
frained from offering simple answers and instead just sat with me in my
pain. My mom was struggling with her own grief that year after her best
friend, Vicki, passed away after a nineteen-year battle with breast cancer.
"I don't know why this happened to John," my mother said to me as we
cried together. "I don't know why Vicki died. I don't know why John is
in a coma. I believe that God is good and that he is in control, but sometimes things just don't seem to make any sense at all." My mom, like
most moms, has an abundance of advice for any given situation. Yet her
not knowing provided a comfort that she could not have given me with
words of advice.

Anne Lamott tells a story that illustrates the mystery of this kind of
faith in her book *Operating Instructions*. While a friend had her two-year-
old sleeping in an adjoining room on a trip, the child somehow climbed
out of her portable crib and locked herself in the dark room. Despite the
mother's frantic efforts, she could not get the door open. Desperate to
comfort her sobbing, terrified child, she slid her fingers under the door
to hold her child's hand. Eventually, the child got the door open, but Lamott connected with the child's fear and desperation as she struggled to
make sense of another friend's recent cancer diagnosis:

> I keep thinking of that story, how much it feels like I'm the two-
> year-old in the dark and God is the mother and I don't speak the
> language. She could break down the door if that struck her as be-
> ing the best way, and ride off with me on her charger. But instead,
> via my friends and my church and my shabby faith, I can just hold
> onto her fingers underneath the door. It isn't enough, and it is.[5]

---

[5]Anne Lamott, *Operating Instructions: A Journal of My Son's First Year* (New York: Anchor Books,
2005), p. 221.

Lamott's words describe my own struggle with pain I cannot understand or explain. I too feel like a child alone in the dark. I want to find my way into the light, but I do not know the way.

When pain and suffering lead us to doubt our faith, we can cling to the one who stands in our place. It is by grace through faith that we are saved, but it also by grace that we grow and heal and learn of God. And when we doubt, it is by grace that we find faith to make it through. As theologian T. F. Torrance writes, "Jesus Christ in me believes in my place and at the same time takes up my poor faltering and stumbling faith in his—'Lord, I believe, help my unbelief'—embracing, upholding and undergirding it through his invariant faithfulness. That is the kind of faith which will never fail."[6] When we are faithless, Jesus is faithful. And we can trust him with our own doubts and fears and questions.

In spite of my earnest efforts, I have never found a satisfying answer to the *why* of John's accident. But somehow, in the midst of my searching, I caught a glimpse of God's fingers under the door and learned that God is bigger than my doubts and fears. This glimpse of God's fingers is a gift of grace. Altson describes her own journey of grace toward a God who can handle her doubts:

> he does not dwell among the petty scripture quotations and the "be thankful in everythings" and the pat answers that bring nothing but guilt and shame and confusion. rather he lives in every "why?" i ask, in every moment i am afraid, in every part of my heart that dares to be honest with him.[7]

Altson describes a God who seeks us and loves us as we really are. This God does not ask us to put on a happy face when our hearts are broken. Rather, he meets us in our whys and fears, our questions and our doubts. Ultimately, this is what happened to me. I found God present in my

---

[6]T. F. Torrance, *The Mediation of Christ* (Grand Rapids: Eerdmans, 1983), p. 108. See also James Torrance, *Worship, Community & the Triune God of Grace* (Downers Grove, Ill.: InterVarsity Press, 1996), pp. 14-18.
[7]Altson, *Stumbling Toward Faith*, p. 98.

deepest moments of fear and doubt. By God's grace, I discovered my own "shabby faith" through John's accident—a faith that God is sovereign and that God is good, even when I do not understand how that is working itself out in the world around me.

Brennan Manning writes, "Often trust begins on the far side of despair. When all human resources are exhausted, when the craving for reassurance is stifled, when we forgo control, when we cease trying to manipulate God and demystify Mystery, then—at our wits' end—trust happens within us."[8] No matter how much I used my intellectual resources, I could not come up with a reason for why the accident happened to John. Regardless of my desire to change the situation, the hard truth was that there was nothing I could do to make John physically better. But ultimately, on the far side of despair, trust happened within me. This may not be a satisfactory explanation to someone else, but it is the only honest one. Through the brokenness I experienced as a result of John's accident, I discovered a trust and a belief in God that was more radical and honest than I had ever known before.

GOD USES OUR BROKENNESS

One of the gifts of brokenness, therefore, is that it can make us honest about our need; it can lead us to a radical openness and trust in God. Another gift of brokenness is that God can redeem and use it. And he does use it. God uses our pain to grow and mature us in him, and he also uses our pain to allow us to reach out to others. Reflect for a moment on times of pain in your own life. When you are hurting, do you seek the counsel and comfort of a friend with a seemingly charmed life who always has everything together? Not me. When I am in pain, I want to talk to someone who knows what it feels like to be hurting. "Only someone who has been there, who has drunk the dregs of our cup of pain, who has experienced the existential loneliness and alienation of the human

---

[8]Brennan Manning, *Ruthless Trust: The Ragamuffin's Path to God* (New York: HarperCollins, 2000), p. 117.

condition, dares whisper the name of the Holy to our unspeakable distress," Manning writes.[9] When I feel lost and alone, I long for the companionship of a kindred spirit—someone who will understand and speak to my broken condition.

Several years ago I counseled a thirty-year-old woman, Caitlyn, who had lost a baby. Just weeks before her due date, Caitlyn discovered that her baby boy had died in the womb, and she had to be induced to deliver her stillborn son. As I sat with Caitlyn, mourning the loss of her baby, my heart broke for her. We worked together for several months, and as Caitlyn moved forward on her grief journey, we said goodbye to one another. Several years later when I had a miscarriage, Caitlyn's experience and words haunted me. Although I did not experience the trauma of delivering a stillborn child, I was broken all the same. Loving friends encouraged me in numerous ways, but Caitlyn's words and feelings came back to me over and over again. This woman who had been my client, whom I had "counseled," whom I had not seen or spoken to for years, ministered to me. Caitlyn has no idea, but God used her broken experience in my life years later. This does not mean God allowed Caitlyn to lose her baby *so that* he could use that in my life. This is a very different thing, and it just means that God *does* use brokenness. Pain and hurt and broken experiences are a result of the fallen state of our world. But God is a God of redemption, and he redeems our suffering.

In the story of Jesus and the hemorrhaging woman, God used her broken experience as well. He used her brokenness to display his healing power. It does not get any more redemptive than that. Yet God has also used this woman's brokenness in a more personal way in my own life. Before Jesus healed her, he looked at this woman and called her "daughter." In a society that often undervalued women, Jesus addressed a woman as "daughter." Those words are healing and tender, and I hear them for me. I too am unclean. This woman's wounds are a source of healing to me and inspire me to fall at Jesus' feet in my own brokenness.

---

[9]Ibid., p. 45.

They remind me that Jesus sees me in my pain and fear and shame and calls me "daughter." God does not promise us a pain-free life, and although God is able to heal us immediately and totally, he does not always do this. But he walks with us and tenderly calls us his daughters, and one day, when we meet our Savior face to face, we will experience final and complete healing.

BROKENNESS NEEDS REAL COMPASSION

The hemorrhaging woman teaches us that brokenness can make us honest about our need and that God can and does use our brokenness. She also illustrates the importance of real compassion when faced with the brokenness in other people's lives. Jesus' choice to heal her, emotionally and physically, is a clear example of his compassion. However, he also demonstrated compassion in his choice to disregard two religious laws: he allowed a woman to touch him, and he spoke to a woman in public. It was Jesus who asked the question of who touched him, yet Jesus in his deity is omnipotent. He knew who touched him! When Jesus asked this question, he invited the woman to speak. In doing so, he revealed that he allowed a woman to touch him. Even worse, the woman was unclean, but Jesus did not appear to feel compelled to go and cleanse himself. Jesus then allowed and invited her to speak in public, and he spoke back to her. Jesus did not respond to this woman as the religious leaders and people of his day would have. Instead, he treated her suffering with infinite compassion.

While I do believe that Christ can choose to heal us physically and emotionally today, I do not generally find that I have the ability to immediately provide people with physical and emotional healing with my words like Jesus did with the bleeding woman. Therefore, what can we learn from Christ's example about how to respond with compassion to broken people? It might seem that we should offer hurting people what we have learned about brokenness here: that pain can lead us to be radically open to God and that God can and does use us in our pain. However, the paradox of true compassion leads us to a different response.

Although I might be tempted to share these truths as a therapist, the

STRONGER THAN YOU THINK

most compassionate response is often a much quieter one. Romans 12:15 tells us to "mourn with those who mourn," but it is important to notice what this passage does not say. It does not say we should try to help mourners understand why they are mourning. It does not say we should explain why God is allowing them to experience their suffering. It does not say we should remind them that God is sovereign and in control. It does not say we should quote Romans 8:28: "In all things God works for the good of those who love him, who have been called according to his purpose." No, Paul says we should *mourn* with those who *mourn*.

Years after C. S. Lewis had written his famous theological exploration of the problem of pain, his own wife died. Initially published under a pseudonym, Lewis wrote another book about pain, *A Grief Observed*, but this one focused on the personal rather than the philosophical:

> Meanwhile, where is God? This is one of the most disquieting symptoms. When you are happy, so happy that you have no sense of needing Him, so happy that you are tempted to feel His claims upon you as an interruption, if you remember yourself and turn to Him with gratitude and praise, you will be—or so it feels—welcomed with open arms. But go to Him when your need is desperate, when all other help is vain and what do you find? A door slammed in your face, and a sound of bolting and double bolting on the inside. After that, silence. You may as well turn away. The longer you wait, the more emphatic the silence will become.[10]

These are the words of a man who is unmistakably lost in pain. Imagine, for a moment, that Lewis sought the counsel of a friend after his wife died. Upon hearing Lewis's anger and frustration, what if that friend began reciting Scriptures or even quoting Lewis's own works? What if he chose to remind Lewis that God is sovereign, or suggested that it was God's timing to take his wife, or maybe that God loved her so much he wanted her home with him? I am guessing Lewis would have been frus-

---

[10]C. S. Lewis, *A Grief Observed* (San Francisco: Harper San Francisco, 2001), p. 9.

trated and dissatisfied with these responses—and with good reason. In the pain-filled words of *A Grief Observed,* Lewis reminds us that when our own lives are struck with tragedy, our perspective changes.

There is compassion in *not* assuring a hurting person it will get better or that time will heal—which we do not know. It may not get better, and time may not heal in the way we think it will.

There is power and compassion in simply sitting with someone in pain, in not rushing her through it. When we tell her everything is going to be okay, this is not really for the hurting individual. Rather, it is often because we are uncomfortable. We want her to pull herself together, and these words hurry her along. When we feel helpless listening to a friend's pain, we should remember that she probably feels helpless too. We can learn from her if we allow ourselves to really listen.

There is compassion in *not* giving advice. There is compassion in *not* trying to fix it. If we insist on being fixers, we do not allow people to come to us with pain that cannot be fixed. When we offer advice, it is usually more for us than for the hurting person; we want him to stop complaining. We do not know what to do with the painful silence, and so we fill it with suggestions. It fills the space, and if he follows our advice, then we believe we have helped. If he chooses to ignore our suggestions, then we can relieve our guilt by telling ourselves that we did our part. The rest is up to him.

Real compassion requires gentleness, honesty and patience. When I choose not to offer advice or even Scripture to a broken person, it is not because of unbelief. I do believe that God is sovereign and that he works things together for good. However, I also believe that when people are lost in pain, I can be Christ's hands and feet most effectively by truly mourning with them—sitting silently and respectfully with them in their pain.

I opened this chapter with my friend John's story, in part because it was one of my first experiences with brokenness. But I also told that story because it is a real story of real pain. I would love to tell you that John was miraculously healed and physically restored in some extraordinary prayer service. Although there has been progress and growth, it has been over a decade since that horrible day when John fell 150 feet in the mountains of Lake Tahoe. He still cannot speak or swallow, and his story does not have what most people would call a "happy" ending. The facts of John's story are sad and painful.

After John's accident, many people said well-meaning but hurtful things to those who loved him. "Maybe God is using this to bring his family closer together." "God allowed this to happen so he could heal him and John could be a testimony to others." "This is all for good; remember Romans 8:28." I remember feeling so guilty that someone quoting Scripture could make me so angry. I felt like I must be a horrible Christian.

In the middle of all those responses, which sent me deeper into my anger and sadness, however, was a friend whose words and actions touched me deeply. I met him about a year after John's accident. He had been a high school friend of John's, but he had gotten heavily involved in drugs in college. At the time I met him, he had been sober for several months and had radically turned his life over to God. When he heard about what had happened to John, he did not say much. He certainly did not say anything profound, and it was what he did *not* say that helped me.

He asked if he could visit John with me. One afternoon the next week, we drove to the nursing home where John was at, and we talked to John and prayed over him. That guy, who was not a close friend and whose name I do not even remember, helped me in my journey. He affected me because he was present to me in my pain. He was honest, and he allowed me to be honest about how awful and confusing and sad it was. He did not offer an easy answer, to me or to John's family, because there is no easy answer. Instead, he met me where I was, in all my fear and sadness and confusion.

That friend was Jesus to me that day. Jesus came to earth to meet us where we are at, and he took on our bodily form, our sin and our brokenness. "Who can take away suffering without entering it?" Henri Nouwen asks. "No God can save us except a suffering God."[11] When we are

---

[11]Henri Nouwen, *The Wounded Healer* (New York: Doubleday, 1972), p. 72.

faced with others' unbearable pain, we can choose to quickly offer books or Bible verses, clichés or empty promises. Yet we worship a God who models true compassion in the face of suffering by entering into that suffering in the most powerful way possible. That is the greatest thing we can do in the face of brokenness. Not offer easy answers. Not give quick fixes. Rather, we can do the hard thing and follow Christ's example and *enter in* to the pain.

TOOLS FOR THE JOURNEY

Allow your wounds to be a source of healing. We are all broken. Regardless of our longing for purity and integrity, the reality of our fallen world and our messy lives is that we are broken people. We have hurt others, and we have been hurt. Sometimes the pain we have faced is so unfair and intense that it paralyzes us. One of the paradoxes of brokenness, however, is that God can lead us further along the journey toward wholeness through that pain. This does not mean God immediately and magically makes us feel okay and complete. Rather, through the hard work of growing through pain, we find that God can turn our "ashes to beauty" (Isaiah 61:3).

During a retreat with Henri Nouwen, Mike Yaconelli reflected on his own woundedness:

> I came to see that it was in my brokenness, in my powerlessness, in my weakness that Jesus was made strong. It was in the acceptance of my lack of faith that God could give me faith. It was in the embracing of my brokenness that I could identify with others' brokenness. It was my role to identify with others' pain, not relieve it.[12]

It is tempting to be a fixer. We want to feel better, and we want to make other people feel better. However, Yaconelli reminds us that we cannot magically relieve other people's hurts. What we can do is be present to

---

[12]As cited in Brennan Manning, *Abba's Child: The Cry of The Heart for Intimate Belonging* (Colorado Springs: NavPress, 1994), p. 52.

them in their pain. We can listen. We can care.

If we allow it to, our own brokenness can teach us how to do this. Begin to pay attention to your wounds, and ask God to show you how he wants to use them as a source of healing. Look for how and where God is working and speaking in the world around you, and then be present. Instead of running from your pains, allow them to teach you. One way to do this is to reflect on how your own wounds have been a source of healing—to you or to others—in your journal. Pray and ask God to reveal to you how he has used your wounds, and then look for new opportunities to let those wounds speak grace and compassion to the people around you. "Making one's own wounds a source of healing, therefore, does not call for a sharing of superficial personal pains," Nouwen writes, "but for a constant willingness to see one's own pain and suffering as rising from the depth of the human condition which all men share."[13] Through our own broken experiences, we can learn to walk gently with others in pain; we can learn how to connect with people in more authentic ways.

Learn to really listen. Imagine that a friend comes to you and discloses that she and her husband have been having marital problems for several years. Recently, she discovered that he has been looking at pornography almost daily. Your friend is overwhelmed with shame and sadness. What are some of the things you might be tempted to say? With genuine concern, you could reassure her: "Everything will be okay. You will work it out. Don't worry; God will get you through it." Or you could ask her questions: "When did this start? How long has he been doing this? Did you have any suspicions? What are you going to do?" Alternatively, you could offer your friend advice: "Why don't you put a parental lock on your computer to keep him from being able to get on those pornography sites? Maybe you two should see a marriage counselor. You know, I like to get new lingerie every few months to keep our sex life exciting. Maybe you could get some new things to spice up your own love life."

---

[13]Nouwen, *Wounded Healer,* p. 88.

Although I suspect genuine truth and care stands behind these words, you can offer your friend something far more powerful in the face of her pain and brokenness. You can listen. Rather than filling the space with reassurances or suggestions or voyeuristic questions, you can be quiet. You can show your friend with your focused attention and silence, your eye contact and body language, that you are there for her. You can communicate love for your friend through being present to her pain. If your friend cries, you can offer a tissue without rushing her through it. If you become uncomfortable, learn from that. Allow that discomfort to give you a tiny window into the horrific pain your friend is experiencing. Rather than running from that discomfort, embrace it. Allow it to be a teacher. You can handle a bit of discomfort to be Christ's hands and feet to your friend.

There is a time and a place for reassurance and suggestions, but too often we rush to those things. Instead, be slow with your speaking. Give your friend plenty of time and space to hurt and grieve. When we are overwhelmed with pain, reassurances can feel empty and silencing. More than advice or reassurances, we need partners on our journey. Learn to be a real listener and force yourself to sit with silence. In doing so, you offer a hurting friend the greatest gift you have: the gift of your companionship.

Reflect on your own journey. Part of wholeness is joining with Christ in his sufferings and then inviting God to use your own wounds to reach a broken world. Instead of running from or trying to avoid pain and suffering, the journey toward wholeness embraces and asks how we can learn from and grow through broken experiences.

Use your journal to reflect on what you have learned through reading this book in your journey toward wholeness:

- How would you have described yourself as the beginning of this journey?
- How have you changed or grown as you have examined your thoughts and voice, your emotions and body image, your self-esteem and relationships, your sexuality and relational wounds?

- As you have explored these things, what have you learned about your own wounds?
- Where are your most broken places?
- Do you feel like you are running from those tender spots, or are you allowing them to be a part of you and to inform your service?
- Brennan Manning writes, "Anyone God uses significantly is always deeply wounded."[14] In what ways has God used your wounded places?

Paul was a deeply wounded person, and he describes the mystery of God working in our brokenness in this way:

> But he said to me, "My grace is sufficient for you, for my power is made perfect in weakness." Therefore, I will boast all the more gladly about my weaknesses, so that Christ's power may rest on me. That is why, for Christ's sake, I delight in weaknesses, in insults, in hardships, in persecutions, in difficulties. For when I am weak, then I am strong. (2 Corinthians 12:9-10)

We do not worship a God who expects us to get things together before we can come to him. Rather, we seek a God who saved us and sought us while we were broken and sinful and messy. Allow that God to draw you into his embrace. Be honest with God, and allow him to help you be honest with other people so that your own wounds can be a source of healing—for yourself and for others. Be amazed at the mystery of God: that in your brokenness you are being made whole. Who you are is not who you have been or what you have had done to you; who you are is who you are becoming in Christ. Christ holds the future, and his work determines who you will be and become—so join with him and receive the gift of healing and restoration he has already won for you and in you.

---

[14]Manning, *Ruthless Trust,* p. 48.

PART FOUR

Growing in Community

Questions for Discussion and Reflection

A Christian community is therefore a healing community
not because wounds are cured and pains are alleviated,
but because wounds and pains become openings or occasions for a new vision.
Mutual confession then becomes a mutual deepening of hope, and sharing
weakness becomes a reminder to one and all of the coming strength.

HENRI NOUWEN
THE WOUNDED HEALER

As image-bearers of God we have been created for relationship and community. We are not meant to enjoy victories and blessings alone, nor are we meant to struggle through difficulties and challenges in isolation. We bear the imprint of God, and one of the most compelling facets of that imprint is our longing and capacity for intimate connections. As you embark on this journey toward the wholeness that God created you with, let me strongly discourage you from trying to make this journey alone. Allow someone else to walk alongside you: to try out the "Tools for the Journey" suggestions with you, to question those things that seem frustrating or confusing, to grieve the painful memories this journey elicits and to encourage you to keep going when you feel like giving up. Community is found among people who can be real with each other and with God—real about the good stuff and the bad stuff. When we are most hurting is when we are most in need of genuine community. Therefore, I encourage you to allow this journey toward wholeness to also be a journey toward community. You may find that they are quite the same.

CHAPTER 1: SEARCHING FOR WHOLENESS IN RELATIONSHIPS, MOTHERHOOD OR CAREER

1. Describe a time when you felt like you just weren't enough or a time when you felt like something was missing or flawed in you.
2. In what ways could you relate to June?
3. Describe how you have chased after the "next thing" at various points in your life. How would you finish the sentence, "I would just be happy if . . ."? For example, I could get married, I could have a(nother) child, my husband would change and so on. In what ways is the thing you're pursuing now keeping you from finding peace?
4. June had a difficult time identifying her strengths. If someone were to give you a piece of paper, could you more quickly write down your strengths or your weaknesses? Where do you think you first learned or heard some of those positive or critical messages?
5. The text mentions some of the negative messages women receive in family relationships, the church and the media. Where have you observed or heard negative messages about what a woman needs to be, do or look like to be a "real" woman? Can you think of other messages about what women should do or be that the text didn't mention that you learned growing up?

CHAPTER 2: FINDING WHOLENESS IN OUR TRUE IDENTITY

1. Describe your church experience growing up. Did you go to church? If not, what did you learn growing up about human nature? Did you learn that we are all basically good or bad? How did these lessons co-

incide with what you observed in the people around you? If you did grow up going to church, what did your church teach you about human nature? Did it emphasize our goodness or badness? How do you think these lessons affected your view of yourself and others?

2. After reading this chapter, what do you think it means to say that we are made in the "image of God"?
3. In what ways could you relate to Lillian in this chapter?
4. Describe how you have grown or changed in and through a relationship (with a significant other, a family member, a friend, God, etc.).

CHAPTER 3: LEARNING TO USE YOUR VOICE

1. How was your experience in school similar to or different from the findings in the study "How Schools Shortchange Girls"?
2. In what ways do you try to please others, perhaps restricting your voice, in order to gain acceptance?
3. The text describes filters we use that keep us from speaking our true thoughts. What filters do you use?
4. Are you more of a yes-sayer or a no-sayer? How do you think this affects your relationships or sense of self-confidence?
5. Describe a time where it worked out well when you were able to tell someone your honest feelings. If sharing your feelings directly or being confrontational is difficult for you, how did you feel or think differently that allowed you to do this?
6. Can you identify a fear or concern you might have about trying some of the "Tools for the Journey" suggestions in this chapter? Talk a little bit about those fears or concerns.

CHAPTER 4: NEGATIVE SELF-TALK

1. If someone else could listen in to your self-talk, what would they hear? Describe a few of the repetitive comments you hear in a typical day. Are they similar to or different from Julie's negative comments?
2. Several thinking errors or cognitive roadblocks are discussed in this

chapter. Which of these do you most engage in? Give an example of a time when you fell into one of these thinking traps.

3. If you tried the thought-stopping technique, what did you learn about your own thinking patterns?

4. Using a real example of a time you engaged in one of the thinking traps, develop a "challenge list" to reframe your thinking.

5. The text suggests developing some truth cards. What are some of the most important truths for you to fill your mind with in order to combat some of the thinking traps you most often fall into?

CHAPTER 5: WHEN YOUR EMOTIONS GET THE BEST OF YOU

1. What emotions do you have a hard time experiencing or expressing? What do you fear would happen if you were, for example, to get angry (if that is difficult for you)?

2. In what ways have you observed as true in your own life that trust often happens on the other side of despair, as suggested by Brennan Manning?

3. What things about yourself are you tempted to try and hide from God? What would it be like for you to be completely honest and transparent before God?

4. Describe a time when you have felt overwhelmed by sadness, worry or anger. What message could that painful emotion have had for you? In what ways were you able to learn or grow from that pain? If you weren't able to hear that message at the time, what could you learn now from that period of your life?

5. In what ways has pain been a teacher in your life? What practical strategies for coping with painful emotions in the past have helped you (e.g., distraction, movies, etc.) ?

6. When you answered the questions regarding when to seek counseling, did you answer yes to a significant number of the items? Have you ever talked to a professional or pastoral counselor before? If so, describe your experience. What are your fears or thoughts about talk-

ing to a counselor? In what way might counseling be helpful for you?

CHAPTER 6: NEVER GOOD ENOUGH

1. Ask your community partner to respond to the statement: "Tell me about *you.*" Talk to each other about your real selves. Afterward, describe how comfortable or uncomfortable you were answering this question. Why do you think you felt that way? What can you learn through this exercise?

2. In what ways did you connect with Karen's experience? How is your story different? Describe ways in which you have felt like you are never good enough.

3. When you hear people talk about self-esteem, what are your immediate thoughts? If self-esteem simply refers to how we think or feel about ourselves, how would you describe your own self-esteem?

4. Describe your attachment relationship with your parents. How secure was that relationship? What kind of internal working model do you think you developed? In what ways was that modified or changed over time?

5. Sanford and Donovan write, "Long before a child says 'I am . . . (strong, lazy, good at math, especially pretty, funny, good with animals, etc.),' chances are she has heard her parents, teachers, siblings and other important people say 'You are . . . (any of the above)' many, many times."[1] What were you told about yourself growing up (e.g., "You are smart," "You are slow," etc.)? In what ways did these messages influence your self-esteem?

6. What are some of the lessons you picked up about the ideal woman through culture or your church growing up? How did these ideas affect your self-esteem?

7. Imagine putting yourself in the place of one of the women Jesus ministered to. What healing words might Jesus offer you?

---

[1]Linda Tschirhart Sanford and Mary Ellen Donovan, *Women & Self-Esteem: Understanding and Improving the Way We Think and Feel About Ourselves* (New York: Penguin Books, 1985), p. 57.

CHAPTER 7: DOING BATTLE WITH YOUR BODY

1. Describe your own body image. Do you feel as if you are in a "battle with your body" sometimes? If so, how?

2. When was the first time you remember having been critical of your appearance? When was the first time you remember someone else having been critical of your body? How do you think those critical reflections affect how you treat your body now?

3. What are some of the things you take for granted that you can do?

4. The text says, "We are not meant to worship our bodies, ignore them, misuse them or hate them." Which of these things are you most likely to do in relation to your body? When do you think this pattern began, and how would you like for it to change?

5. Describe a practical way you can look at and appreciate your self as a whole this week.

CHAPTER 8: RETHINKING FEMALE SEXUALITY

1. What kinds of lessons or messages did you hear growing up about sex and female sexuality? In what ways did you learn that sex and sexuality are shameful?

2. Have you ever had anyone speak to you or approach you sexually in a way that made you uncomfortable? Have you ever done or said sexual things that you did not feel comfortable with, even if you did not resist or voice your discomfort? What is it like for you to reflect on these memories? In what ways were these things violating to you?

3. In what ways has sexual sin affected your relationship with God, your relationship with yourself, or your relationships with your husband or significant others? Have you allowed yourself to experience the shocking forgiveness and love of Christ? If not, what has kept you from this?

4. If you are single, what was your response to Jane's story? In what ways could you relate to her struggles? How have you coped with your God-given sexual urges and longing for intimate connection? If you

are married, what did you learn about the struggles single women face? In what ways can you foster more informed intimacy and connection with single women?

CHAPTER 9: THE SEARCH FOR CONNECTION

1. In what ways have you restricted, ignored or suppressed aspects of yourself in order to maintain relationships with others? The author writes, "Some of us become so intent on finding intimacy that we will do anything to keep relationships, even if we lose our very selves in the process." What things have you done to find "intimacy" in the past?

2. If healthy relationships begin with people who know and respect themselves, where would you describe yourself in that process? How well do you know yourself? How well do you respect yourself?

3. Reflect on how easy or difficult it is for you to maintain direct relationships. How have triangulation and passive-aggressive behavior affected your relationships? How can you cultivate more direct relationships in your life—with friends or coworkers, siblings or in-laws, spouses or parents?

4. Describe your experience with female competition. Talk about what that was like and how it has affected your female relationships.

5. Do you tend to be a fixer? When you get in relationships, how much do you try to advise, save or help the other person? What is it like for you to step out of that role and just *be* with another person?

6. What relationships do you have that you struggle to allow the other person to truly be himself or herself? What do you suspect you might be missing in this? What are some of the unique gifts and talents and peculiarities of that person that you might not be experiencing because of this?

7. What is it like for you to affirm others? Does this seem threatening or uncomfortable? Did you grow up hearing an excess or lack of affirmation from your parents?

8. Would significant others describe you as being somewhat passive or dependent? Or, on the other hand, would significant others in your life describe you as more controlling or dominant? As you reflect on your current relationships, is it more difficult for you to *be* a whole person, or to invite *others* to be whole in relationships? In what ways can you begin to grow toward wholeness in these challenging areas?

CHAPTER 10: RESTORING YOUR BROKEN HEART

1. Reflect on your own heart. In what ways have you been hurt or wounded in relationships? If relational wounds are like a knife in the chest, describe that knife for you. How deeply is it planted in your chest? Have you tried to remove it? What kinds of scars have been left behind?

2. Have you ever really told the story of your deepest relational wound? If not, I would encourage you to use this community relationship to do just that. Choose a safe person, time and place, where you will have ample space and opportunity to do whatever you need to do—cry, yell, hug, scream, throw something or sit quietly—as long as you tell your story. Acknowledge the depth of your woundedness, and let the telling be a step toward healing.

3. When you consider cleaning out your relational wounds, what kinds of harmful relational patterns do you observe in your life? In what ways have bitterness and resentment affected your current relationships?

4. What is it like for you to think about forgiveness? Do you quickly and immediately endorse your need to and ability to forgive? Forgiveness of real pain is not easy. If it feels simple and easy, then perhaps you have not fully acknowledged the depth of your pain. On the other hand, does even the thought of forgiveness make your mouth go dry and your stomach churn? In order to move toward new growth, who do you most need to forgive? If forgiveness is a process, where are you in that process?

CHAPTER 11: WHOLLY BROKEN . . . YET STILL WHOLE

1. Reflect for a moment on times when you have been hurting. Describe a season of brokenness in your own life. When you were hurting, what responses were most helpful to you? Did you have people who were present to you in your pain? On the other hand, did you have people offer you pat answers and advice? How did the various responses to your pain affect you?

2. In what ways have seasons of brokenness affected your faith in God? Have those times made you deeply aware of your need for something beyond yourself, or have you experienced something different? How have you struggled with your faith in those broken times? How can you allow Christ to step in and hold your faith for you?

3. In what ways have other people's experiences of pain been healing to you? How have you seen God use your own brokenness in other people's lives?

4. How have you responded to hurting people in the past? In your genuine care and concern for others, how often have you given advice or offered quick reassurances? What is it like for you to contemplate a quieter response to other people's pain? Does the feeling of helplessness with that response seem overwhelming? How can that helpless feeling increase your compassion?

5. What is most challenging for you as you consider entering into people's pain when they are hurting? What is it like for you to contemplate the painful task of entering into other people's suffering?

As you continue on your own journey toward wholeness, let me echo Paul's words and leave you with this prayer:

> I pray that the eyes of your heart may be enlightened in order that you may know the hope to which he has called you, the riches of his glorious inheritance in his people, and his incomparably great power for us who believe. That power is the same as the mighty

strength he exerted when he raised Christ from the dead and seated him at his right hand in the heavenly realms. (Ephesians 1:18-20)

Remember that you are a precious child made in God's image—that is who you are. Remember also "the hope to which he has called you"—that the image of God is who you are and who you are becoming. And trust that, by grace, Jesus is standing in the gap, empowering you to live responsively and responsibly in your journey toward wholeness.

Further Reading

CHAPTER 1: SEARCHING FOR WHOLENESS IN ROMANCE, MOTHERHOOD OR CAREER

Bilezikian, Gilbert. *Beyond Sex Roles: What the Bible Says About a Woman's Place in Church and Family.* 2nd ed. Grand Rapids: Baker Books, 1985.

Fischer, Kathleen. *Women at the Well: Feminist Perspectives on Spiritual Direction.* New York: Paulist, 1988.

Grenz, Stanley, and Denise Muir Kjesbo. *Women in the Church: A Biblical Theology of Women in Ministry.* Downers Grove, Ill.: InterVarsity Press, 1995.

Hubbard, M. Gay. *Women: The Misunderstood Majority.* Dallas: Word, 1992.

Manning, Brennan. *Abba's Child: The Cry of the Heart for Intimate Belonging.* Colorado Springs: NavPress, 1994.

Van Leeuwen, Mary Stewart. *Gender & Grace: Love, Work and Parenting in a Changing World.* Downers Grove, Ill.: InterVarsity Press, 1990.

CHAPTER 2: FINDING WHOLENESS IN OUR TRUE IDENTITY

Balswick, Jack O., Pamela Ebstyne King and Kevin S. Reimer. *The Reciprocating Self: Human Development in Theological Perspective.* Downers Grove, Ill.: InterVarsity Press, 2005.

Grenz, Stanley. *The Social God and the Relational Self: A Trinitarian Theology of the Imago Dei.* Louisville, Ky.: Westminster John Knox Press, 2001.

Gunton, Colin E. *The Promise of Trinitarian Theology.* Edinburgh: T & T Clark, 1991.

Hoekema, Anthony. *Created in God's Image.* Grand Rapids: Eerdmans, 1986.

Lewis, C. S. *Mere Christianity*. San Francisco: HarperSanFrancisco, 2001.

Manning, Brennan. *Ruthless Trust: The Ragamuffin's Path to God*. New York: HarperCollins, 2000.

Plantinga, Cornelius, Jr. *Not the Way It's Supposed to Be: A Breviary of Sin*. Grand Rapids: Eerdmans, 1995.

Torrance, Thomas F. *The Mediation of Christ*. Grand Rapids: Eerdmans, 1983.

CHAPTER 3: LEARNING TO USE YOUR VOICE

McMinn, Lisa Graham. *Growing Strong Daughters: Encouraging Girls to Become All They're Meant to Be*. Grand Rapids: Baker Books, 2000.

Orenstein, Peggy. *Schoolgirls: Young Women, Self-Esteem and the Confidence Gap*. New York: Anchor, 1994.

Pipher, Mary. *Reviving Ophelia: Saving the Selves of Adolescent Girls*. New York: Ballantine, 1994.

Shandler, Sara. *Ophelia Speaks: Adolescent Girls Write About Their Search for Self*. New York: HarperPerennial, 1999.

CHAPTER 4: NEGATIVE SELF-TALK

Burns, David. *Feeling Good: The New Mood Therapy Revised and Updated*. New York: Avon Books, 1999.

Cantor, Dorothy, Carol Goodheart, Sandra Haber, Ellen McGrath, Alice Rubenstein, Lenore Walker, Karen Zager and Andrea Thompson. *Finding Your Voice: A Woman's Guide to Using Self-Talk for Fulfilling Relationships, Work, and Life*. Hoboken, N.J.: Wiley, 2004.

Greenberger, Dennis, and Christine Padesky. *Mind Over Mood: Change How You Feel by Changing the Way You Think*. New York: Guilford, 1995.

CHAPTER 5: WHEN YOUR EMOTIONS GET THE BEST OF YOU

Bourne, Edmund J. *The Anxiety & Phobia Workbook*. 4th ed. Oakland, Calif.: New Harbinger Publications, 2005.

Derosis, Helen. *Women & Anxiety: A Step-by-Step Program for Managing Anxiety and Depression.* Rev. ed. Long Island City, N.Y.: Hatherleigh Press, 1998.

Frankel, Lois. *Women, Anger & Depression: Strategies for Self-Empowerment.* Deerfield Beach, Fla.: Health Communications, 1991.

Hart, Archibald, and Catherine Hart Weber. *Unveiling Depression in Women: A Practical Guide to Understanding and Overcoming Depression.* Grand Rapids: Revell, 2002.

Lerner, Harriet Goldhor. *The Dance of Anger: A Woman's Guide to Changing the Patterns of Intimate Relationships.* New York: Harper & Row, 1985.

Yancey, Philip. *Where Is God When It Hurts?* Grand Rapids: Zondervan, 1990.

CHAPTER 6: NEVER GOOD ENOUGH

Benner, David. *The Gift of Being Yourself: The Sacred Call to Self-Discovery.* Downers Grove, Ill.: InterVarsity Press, 2004.

McGee, Robert. *The Search For Significance: Seeing Your True Worth Through God's Eyes.* Nashville: W Publishing Group, 2003.

Palmer, Parker. *Let Your Life Speak: Listening for the Voice of Vocation.* San Francisco: Jossey-Bass, 2000.

Sanford, Linda Tschirhart, and Mary Ellen Donovan. *Women and Self-Esteem: Understanding and Improving the Way We Think and Feel About Ourselves.* New York: Penguin Books, 1985.

CHAPTER 7: DOING BATTLE WITH YOUR BODY

Cash, Thomas F. *The Body Image Workbook: An 8-Step Program for Learning to Like Your Looks.* Oakland, Calif.: New Harbinger Publications, 1997.

Franklin, Regina. *Who Calls Me Beautiful: Finding Our True Image in the Mirror of God.* Grand Rapids: Discovery House, 2004.

Graham, Michelle. *Wanting to Be Her: Body Image Secrets Victoria Won't Tell You.* Downers Grove, Ill.: InterVarsity Press, 2005.

Lamott, Anne. *Traveling Mercies: Some Thoughts on Faith*. New York: Pantheon Books, 1999.

Maine, Margo, and Joe Kelly. *The Body Myth: Adult Women and the Pressure to Be Perfect*. Hoboken, N.J.: Wiley, 2005.

CHAPTER 8: RETHINKING FEMALE SEXUALITY

Hart, Archibald, Catherine Hart Weber and Debra Taylor. *Secrets of Eve*. Nashville: Word Publishing, 1998.

McMinn, Lisa Graham. *Sexuality and Holy Longing: Embracing Intimacy in a Broken World*. San Francisco: Jossey-Bass, 2004.

Rosenau, Douglas E. *A Celebration of Sex: A Guide to Enjoying God's Gift of Sexual Intimacy*. Nashville: Thomas Nelson, 1994.

Smedes, Lewis. *Sex for Christians: The Limits and Liberties of Sexual Living*. Grand Rapids: Eerdmans, 1976.

Wheat, Ed, and Gaye Wheat. *Intended for Pleasure: Sex Technique and Sexual Fulfillment in Christian Marriage*. 3rd ed. Grand Rapids: Revell, 1997.

Sexual Abuse

Allender, Dan. *The Wounded Heart*. Colorado Springs: NavPress, 1990.

Bass, Ellen, and Laura Davis. *The Courage to Heal*. New York: HarperPerennial, 1988.

Maltz, Wendy. *The Sexual Healing Journey*. New York: Harper, 2001.

Sexual Addictions

Arterburn, Stephen. *Every Man's Battle: Winning the War on Sexual Temptation One Victory at a Time*. Colorado Springs: WaterBrook Press, 2000.

Hall, Laurie. *An Affair of the Mind*. Wheaton, Ill.: Tyndale, 1996.

Means, Marsha. *Living with Your Husband's Secret Wars*. Grand Rapids: Revell, 1999.

Schaumburg, Harry W. *False Intimacy: Understanding the Struggle of Sexual Addiction*. Colorado Springs: NavPress, 1997.

Singles

Courtney, Camerin. *Table for One: The Savvy Girl's Guide to Singleness.* Grand Rapids: Revell, 2002.

Hsu, Albert Y. *Singles at the Crossroads: A Fresh Perspective on Christian Singleness.* Downers Grove, Ill.: InterVarsity Press, 1997.

McDonald, Skip. *And She Lived Happily Ever After: Finding Fulfillment as a Single Woman.* Downers Grove, Ill.: InterVarsity Press, 2005.

Muto, Susan Annette. *Celebrating the Single Life: A Spirituality for Single Persons in Today's World.* New York: Image Books, 1985.

CHAPTER 9: THE SEARCH FOR CONNECTION

Balswick, Jack O., and Judith K. Balswick. *A Model for Marriage: Covenant, Grace, Empowerment and Intimacy.* Downers Grove, Ill.: IVP Academic, 2006.

Benner, David. *Sacred Companions: The Gift of Spiritual Friendship and Direction.* Downers Grove, Ill.: InterVarsity Press, 2002.

Lerner, Harriet Goldhor. *The Dance of Intimacy: A Women's Guide to Courageous Acts of Change in Key Relationships.* New York: HarperCollins, 1990.

Schnarch, David. *Passionate Marriage: Keeping Love & Intimacy Alive in Commiitted Relationships.* New York: Owl Books, 1997.

CHAPTER 10: RESTORING YOUR BROKEN HEART

Kübler-Ross, Elisabeth, and David Kessler. *On Grief and Grieving: Finding the Meaning of Grief through the Five Stages of Loss.* New York: Scribner, 2005.

Lewis, C. S. *A Grief Observed.* San Francisco: HarperSanFrancisco, 2001.

———. *The Problem of Pain.* San Francisco: HarperSanFrancisco, 2001.

Smedes, Lewis. *The Art of Forgiving.* New York: Ballantine Books, 1996.

———. *Forgive & Forget.* New York: Simon & Schuster, 1984.

Worthington, Everett. *Forgiving and Reconciling: Bridges to Wholeness and Hope.* Downers Grove, Ill.: InterVarsity Press, 2003.

Zonnebelt-Smeenge, Susan J., and Robert C. DeVries. *Getting to the Other*

Side of Grief: Overcoming the Loss of a Spouse. Grand Rapids: Baker Books, 1999.

CHAPTER 11: WHOLLY BROKEN . . . YET STILL WHOLE

Altson, Renee. *Stumbling Toward Faith.* Grand Rapids: Zondervan, 2004.

Manning, Brennan. *Ragamuffin Gospel: Good News for the Bedraggled, Beat-Up, and Burnt Out.* Portland: Multnomah, 1990.

McMinn, Mark R. *Why Sin Matters: The Surprising Relationship Between Our Sin and God's Grace.* Wheaton, Ill.: Tyndale, 2004.

Nouwen, Henri. *The Wounded Healer.* New York: Doubleday, 1972.

Yancey, Philip. *What's So Amazing About Grace?* Grand Rapids: Zondervan, 2002.

Author Index

4 - -